THE FEARLESS TRAVELER

THE
Fearless Traveler

Tips to get you there and keep you happy

CHARLOTTE BEECH

MQP

MQ Publications Limited
12 The Ivories, 6–8 Northampton Street, London N1 2HY
tel: 020 7359 2244, fax: 020 7359 1616
e-mail: mail@mqpublications.com
www.mqpublications.com

ISBN: 1-84072-553-2

10 9 8 7 6 5 4 3 2 1

Printed in China

Text and cover printed on
100% recycled paper.

Contents

Fearless...

A word from the author

Let me start by coming clean: Although I've traveled far and wide for many years, I'm not naturally a Fearless Traveler. Far from it. Inwardly, I turn to jelly at the merest mention of snakes or parasites, and routinely scour guidebooks for every known exotic disease on the continent. But I know that I'm not alone—the most seasoned travelers get anxious at times—and when you think about it, it's silly not to be just a tad worried about traveling. After all, going abroad means leaving behind everything with which you're familiar and setting off into the great unknown. You'll be coping with new languages, food, cultures, and dangers. What guarantee do you have that you won't be left up the proverbial creek without a paddle?

Ever since I was a teenager I have blundered, tripped, and stumbled my way around the world, finding myself in almost every imaginable pickle, jam, and other sticky mess along the way. I have wrongly deciphered Asian script and happily sauntered into the men's toilets, suffered Delhi-belly, and been told that what I just ate was a goat's intestines. I've found myself swimming with alligators; spat at by mercurial llamas; being ripped off by cunning hagglers; dodging tanks in a South American riot; and literally fishing jungle ants out of my pants.

But the good news is that with each new hiccup comes hindsight and the wisdom of how to avoid troublesome situations. If we all started out equipped with a thorough knowledge of seasoned travelers' pitfalls, gaffes, and slip-ups, couldn't we steer our path more confidently?

Well, that's precisely what this book will do for you. It's an accumulation of my own and other travelers' hindsight, wisdom, hints, and inspirational stories to arm any adventurer setting off into the wide blue yonder. So whether you're planning to scale Mount Everest, lose yourself in the jungle, relax on a cruise ship, or discover the perfect honeymoon location, all the advice, hints, and tips you need to get you there and stay happy once you've arrived are right here. All that remains is to find your passport and toothbrush, and go make those incredible memories that will last you a lifetime.

Charlotte Beech

1 Fearless
Forward planning

"Twenty years from now you will be more disappointed by the things that you didn't do than by the ones you did do. So throw off the bowlines. Sail away from the safe harbor. Catch the trade winds in your sails. Explore. Dream. Discover."

MARK TWAIN

In the fourth century AD, St. Augustine said, "The world is a book and those who do not travel read only one page." And his words still ring true for every fearless traveler. Traveling stimulates and exhilarates, widens your experience, and refreshes your mind. You can experience different cultures and try out new activities that are far removed from your everyday existence. And you'll not only discover things about other places and people, but also about yourself. You can surprise yourself with what you can do. It's a leap into something entirely different, whether you're steaming through an Amazonian rainforest, drifting through the desert sands, or chilling out on a tropical beach.

It's not at all surprising to be nervous before you travel. If you're not a naturally devil-may-care character, then you can gain carefree characteristics through a bit of preparation and research. Advance planning is the best way to allay your anxieties. It might not sound very exciting, but all of us would do well to plan carefully if only to minimize hassles and get the most out of a trip.

If trepidation is stopping you from traveling or is just giving you butterflies, read on to overcome and confront your fears. It would be a shame to regret not doing something just because you're scared.

Don't be put off

Remember that travel almost always sounds more daunting than it is. For one thing, if you listen to other travelers' frequently exaggerated tales, it may begin to sound as if there are snakes up every tree and kidnappers hiding around every corner. I confess that I'm guilty of it, too: I've often told the stories of when I swam in piranha-infested rivers, fed alligators at close quarters, and eyeballed sharks in the sea, but I was never in any real danger—those piranhas hardly ever attacked humans, the alligators were too intent on what I was feeding them to take a snap at me, and the sharks were not man-eaters and only grew about four feet long.

But it's not just travelers' tall tales that give us the jitters. Even day-to-day traveling can seem daunting at first. Before heading to West Africa, I talked to several experienced African travelers. They nonchalantly told me to take a truck over the border to get from Mali to Mauritania. I thought this sounded worrying. How would you find and pay for a ride? Where do you stay? Is it dangerous on your own? In the end I took a deep breath, tried not to think about it, set off, and found that the reason for their nonchalance was that it was easy: people were helpful and the rugged trucks bounced their way across the border regularly. In the end, I couldn't think what I'd been worried about—it was all just a wonderful adventure!

Where and what kind of trip?

The world that you visit is whatever you choose to make it. Before choosing your destination, think about what you want from your trip. Are you in need of restorative calm or reckless excitement? Do you want to go somewhere to take stock, reflect, relax, or to get your senses assaulted and enriched by variety? Do you want strangeness and unfamiliarity, culture shock and discovery, or soothing serenity? Or would you like a heady kaleidoscopic cocktail of these sensations?

You could opt for somewhere exotic or familiar, a spell in a hectic city, exploration in a rainforest, recuperation on the beach, or mountain climbing—whatever does it for you. What relaxes some people would drive others crazy. Some get their kicks from a beach, others from jumping out of planes!

FEARLESS PREPARATION

One of the best ways to banish fears is to research the place where you are going. Learning both practical and background information will prepare you properly and means you'll know what to expect. Finding out about a culture also prevents you from making inadvertent blunders and eases your travel considerably.

Internet: It's easier than ever before to find out about places, thanks to the Internet. You can not only compare prices, book tickets, and find and book hotels, you can also post questions on a travel bulletin board such as Lonely Planet's Thorntree (http://thorntree.lonelyplanet.com). *See* chapter 6 for additional resources.

You might also want to check about the safety of some destinations. The US government publishes up-to-date travel warnings at www.travel.state.gov/travel_warnings.html to keep you informed about their advisories.

Travel clubs: Other resources include travel clubs such as www.globetrotters.co.uk, an organization that's been around for more than 50 years. These clubs can put you in touch with other travelers and serve as an information network. There are also regional travel clubs around the world such as South American Explorers (www.samexplo.org).

Books: Books are a superb way to get a feel for your destination. Guidebooks, travelogues, books on historical and political background, and even fiction can help to create a palpable sense of a place. Newspaper supplements and specialist travel magazines are great for discovering places to go, helpful travel tips, and the latest news.

TV: An effortless means of research is watching travel and documentary TV programs that bring the world into your living room while inspiring you to make that move out of your armchair.

It's also smart to keep an eye on what's happening in the news at your intended destination. This is always worth checking out: in 2002, two Japanese tourists were very disappointed when they tried to visit the Church of the Nativity in Bethlehem—they found it was the 16th day of an Israeli siege on Palestinian gunmen inside!

Travel fairs: Travel fairs are great for inspiration and ideas. They offer talks and displays about various destinations and companies, and you can check out what different travel companies offer as well as develop your own ideas about where to go. You can often find out about special offers and big discounts at these fairs, too. Running searches on the Internet can usually help find the travel fairs nearest to you.

When and for how long?

Planning your itinerary is as important as choosing your destination. So would you like to stay put somewhere for a while or do your itchy feet keep you on the move? Do you like the thrills and spills of moving quickly and covering as much ground as possible? Or would you rather take things a little slower and soak up more of what a place has to offer? The wonderful thing about staying in one region is that you'll discover it more deeply—making friends, exploring further, finding out what makes the people there tick. If you travel as if checking off items on a list, you'll miss out—unless lists rock your world, of course. However, traveling fast has its own joys—you get to plunge in and out of places, sampling the variety of what's there. Contrast and culture shock are exciting in themselves. So give some thought to your own energy supplies and the extent of your wanderlust, and you'll tailor the perfect travel plan for yourself.

Taking the plunge

Once you've decided where you want to go, you can decide how to go about it. Arranging your trip independently works out to be less expensive and more flexible most of the time than working through a tour service or travel agency. But how much time do you have? If you don't want to organize the trip yourself, there is a whole industry out there raring to do it for you. For example, if you want to take a totally stress-free holiday, go for an all-inclusive package that absolves you of any responsibilities. But in addition to more conventional tours, there are adventurous yet structured options such as overland trips—where you might cross Africa or South America in a converted truck with experienced guides. A full list of overland companies is given at www.go-overland.com.

Work or learn abroad

Rather than traveling just for pleasure, you could go abroad to work, study, or volunteer. This can be a great way of gaining a completely different experience and extending your time away. Many companies exist to help you find these opportunities. Options include teaching English, working as a tour guide, picking fruit, waiting tables, crewing a yacht, looking after children, doing bar work, or working in a ski resort.

If you settle in an area to do voluntary work, you're much more likely to see beyond the surface of a culture while doing something to help the community or environment of the place you are visiting. One good thing about doing voluntary work, apart from the fuzzy glow it gives you inside, is that it doesn't necessarily have to be a long-term project—every little bit counts. You can often put in only as much time and effort as you can easily spare. For example, I did just a week's work in the Ecuadorian wilderness clearing jungle paths and assisting with the upkeep of an eco-travel institution. However, there are also plenty of institutions that are in desperate need of long-term volunteers.

Fearless and peerless

Going it alone can seem like the most daunting prospect. A strange place populated by strangers doesn't always sound like a recipe for a lot of fun. But traveling alone can be a fantastic way to go. Lone travelers tend to mix more, because you are not only forced to be more outgoing, but are also more approachable. You never have to go along with anyone else's plan and can do exactly as you please, which makes being on your own a refreshingly free way to be.

The disadvantages are that you don't have anyone to help you make difficult decisions. You will be lonely from time to time and will have to deal with this. If you're ill, you won't have anyone to bring you bottled water and sympathy.

Traveling alone can also provide the most magical and unexpected experiences. When I was in Calcutta, India, I befriended a young Indian couple who were amazed that I was traveling on my own. They took me under their wing and spent the next few days giving me an extraordinary insight into the city and visiting all the least-touristed places. They took me to a craft "village" where preparations for the upcoming festival of Durga Puja were under way; we walked through long passageways of artisans painting innumerable sparkling idols for the thousands of shrines being erected across the city.

I accompanied the wife to the traditional ceremonies to make offerings to the idols and was pulled into the ceremony by being smeared with colorful powders and tasting the exquisite sweets given as gifts. My new friends also knew the best spot to see the climax of the festival. So we took our place at the riverbank in the evening and watched, in the fading light of the sunset, as the thousands of lovingly made and displayed idols were carried in dancing, whirling processions. The idols were brought to the river's edge and submerged under the dark waters—all to the rhythm of wild, pounding drums. It was an unforgettable experience, and it would never have been the same if I had not been traveling solo.

Fearless women

Don't be put off because you're a woman alone. I've traveled a lot on my own—in Europe, South America, and Asia—and have found that the random kindnesses and protectiveness of strangers far outweigh the mosquito-like irritation of harassment from men. I was once stranded in an Amazonian village with a tropical storm raging. The rain was coming down so hard, I couldn't see a thing. The village had no hotels and no buses were running because the rain had washed away sections of the dirt road. I was seriously considering huddling down in a pew of the local church for the night, when up came a cheerful local woman—all smiles. She promptly invited me to stay at her house, where she fed me, chatted merrily and gave me a warm bed for what turned out to be several days before the roads were passable. We are still in contact, and happily, that's not unique—I have dozens more stories from all around the world of similar kindnesses shown to me as a solo traveler. *See* p. 94 for some tips for female travelers.

Finding your perfect partner

If you're worried about going it alone but can't find anyone with whom to go, you could join an organized overland trip, do a course or organized activity, or even advertise for a like-minded companion in a magazine or on the Net. But don't panic if your search is fruitless. You'll often meet people along the way on long-haul trips and end up traveling with them for at least part of the way. Sometimes they are more experienced than you and can help you make the most of your travels with insider information.

Double trouble

Going with one other person is a companiable way to travel. It's great to have a buddy—not only do you have someone to guard your bags while you go to the bathroom, you also have someone to share experiences with, commiserate with when things go wrong, and after the trip, to share memories. It's also cheaper to travel with someone else because you can share accommodation costs.

Problems can happen with even your nearest and dearest. I once traveled to Crete with my brother, who quickly relaxed and was happy to take life slowly during the day and live the high life in the evenings. I was more hyperactive during the day and couldn't match his late-night energy. After a week of my dragging him out of bed at 7:00 a.m. and into the nearest archeological site or gorge walk, followed by his taking me for an all-nighter, we realized that something had to give.

The super group

Traveling in a group can be the most fun way to go. A party atmosphere is more likely when there are more than two of you, and it's not as intense as traveling in a pair. Another boon is that traveling in a group brings costs down even further.

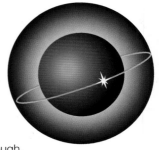

Group dynamics can be interesting though, and it's much more difficult to make decisions. I went to Mexico with a group of friends. It was good fun, but it took us so long to make decisions that we realized we were missing out on valuable adventure-making time. So we split into two groups of three and traveled separately for a few weeks, then met up again to relax on the beach—there, the biggest decision was who was going to get the beer!

However, going away with someone is also a test of your relationship. You'll probably be spending a lot more intensive time together than you have before. As Mark Twain once put it, "I have found out that there ain't no surer way to find out whether you like people or hate them than to travel with them." You'll discover how each of you behaves under stress, how to cope with each person's expectations about the trip, and how to work out compromises from time to time.

FEARLESS TICKET BUYING

The cheapest tickets are usually available if you book in advance. You can save yourself serious amounts of money by researching the best route. Also, look for special deals—some airlines offer great discounts to students and senior citizens.

Round the world

Buying a Round-the-World ticket can work out to be very inexpensive and is an amazing way to cover a lot of ground. The world's contrasts are brought into sharp relief and you can experience the planet's sheer diversity by pinging from place to place. The downside is that you can end up moving too quickly, and be unable to spend enough time in any one place to absorb what you are seeing. The best idea is to go for flexibility so that you can settle as the mood takes you.

Ravishing returns

You can also create an interesting trip with a simple long-haul return ticket by making use of stopovers—you can often arrange to break your journey in an exciting place on the way. Or you could invest in an open-jaw ticket. Open-jaw tickets allow you to fly to one destination and return from another, and are available through many travel services and agencies. They allow you to explore the area between your destination and departure sites—a big advantage for most travelers.

No frills

In Europe, you can book amazingly cheap European fares on no-frills airlines such as Easyjet or Ryanair. In the States, Jet Blue and Southwest fulfill your no-frills needs. Because these airlines sell one-way tickets, it's easy to arrange an open-jaw option. Airlines also publish a newsletter for frequent users— you can get incredible first-come, first-serve deals this way.

Courier flights

You can get some really great deals with courier flights— these are flights you can buy at a discounted price in return for acting as a courier on the flight for a company. Usually the company will ask you to carry documents or use your baggage allowance for their bags, not yours, meaning that you can take only your carry-on luggage. In return for this, you get a much cheaper ticket, and it's usually a return. To get a courier flight, register with the International Association of Air Travel Couriers at www.iaatc.com. The annual fee is $45.

Upgrades

You're most likely to get a free upgrade to a higher class if you're enrolled in the airline's frequent flyer program. If you've been racking up air miles, try cashing them in for an upgrade. You may even get bumped up when the plane is overbooked! It helps if you're alone, well dressed, and don't need a special meal. You're also wise to watch for credit card offers—some cards occasionally have special offers that include upgrades.

Happy families

More and more families are traveling together for a few months or even a year. For children, it can be a fantastic experience and education. For parents who were beginning to wonder if they were getting too settled, it can be a welcome leap into the unknown.

If you are going to be away for a long time, you can teach your children on the road with correspondence courses to prevent their falling behind at school. Taking the whole family means that you don't have to miss the excitement of traveling now that you are responsible for children, and your children will find it an incredible, stimulating experience. They will also help you see things through different eyes and from a new vantage point. Being somewhere with children helps you interact with local people, too.

Be realistic about what kind of trip you can manage. Usually the best kind of holiday with children is to country destinations rather than big-city sightseeing, but these kinds of trips can be really fun.

Money, money, money!

It might be the root of all evil, but it sure helps you get around and have fun. First budget the amount of money you'll need. Add up expected prices for transportation, insurance, visas, vaccinations, and equipment. Then look at how much you'll need from day to day. You can figure this out by getting a guidebook and learning how much your proposed lifestyle will cost, factoring in accommodation, transportation, meals, and entertainment.

Then you'll need to organize your money. It's best to plan for a few different ways to access your funds so you can fall back on one if money in one account dries up or a card is not accepted. Research the best form to take for each country you are going to visit, as well as how much you'll be charged for transactions—for example, cash advances on a credit card. It may be best to take a couple of credit cards in case one is not accepted. You can usually insure your cards with a card protection plan.

If you are taking traveler's checks, verify which currency and company are the best for each destination. Remember to write down the serial numbers of the checks and leave the list with someone at home—and also e-mail it to yourself.

Wise up on ways to withdraw

Find out how to change money in the country you are visiting and take backup. Don't necessarily rely on there being ATMs on every corner. When I was traveling in Mali, it seemed that there was only one ATM in the whole country, and it only accepted VISA—I had Mastercard. I had travelers' checks but I didn't have the receipt for them with me—the bank required this to cash the checks. I ended up having to cash them on the black market outside the bank—sitting in someone's car, which was more exciting than queuing up in the bank, but more risky and definitely offered worse rates of exchange!

Insurance

Fearless or fearful, all travelers need insurance to fall back on. If you fall ill, have an accident, or have something stolen, you will deeply regret not being insured. Traveling without basic insurance is just asking for trouble to be more troublesome than it has to be.

When choosing which insurance to buy, check that you'll be covered for any activities you might be planning. Look at the extra you'll have to pay on the policy and the ceiling on payouts for any valuables you're taking along.

Your credit card may insure some items, so it's worth checking out the small print. For example, if you pay for your airline ticket by credit card, you may be able to get your money back if your ticket is lost in the mail.

Get your shots

You can get vaccines or preventative medicines for many of the world's diseases, so remember to ask your doctor about them. You don't want to develop yellow fever in the middle of your dream trip. Visit your doctor or a travel health center at least six weeks before you set off to learn which vaccinations or anti-malarial medication may be necessary. Requirements for countries change, so it's important to consult informed medical people for the latest information.

If you can't get to the doctor six weeks prior to your trip, try to get there at least three weeks beforehand. That should give enough time to fit in an immunization schedule. Last minute shots are better than none, but remember that you have to have anti-malarial medication at least a week before you leave.

Once you've had your shots, record them on a certificate. Take a copy of the certificate with you so you'll know what you've been protected against. This can be useful if you need medical treatment and may also be required to enter certain countries. For health information, try the World Health Organization at www.who.int.

Be a copy cat

However busy you are in the run-up towards your departure, it's always worth taking the time and trouble to make a good back-up system for yourself. This is specially important when it comes to making duplicate records of documents that you will be taking with you on your travels. Leave photocopies of these important documents with someone at home—this includes your passport, visas, and insurance documents. It's also wise to take photocopies with you, or store details of them on your e-mail address, or in "travel vaults"—*see* p. 149 for information on how to do this. Bring a few extra passport photos along, too; it's not a great hassle to do this in one of those instant photo booths, and you never know when you might need them for visas and other documents.

DOCUMENTS

Passport

You can find out all you ever wanted to know about applying for one of these at http://travel.state.gov. If you don't have a passport, allow at least six weeks to apply for one before you leave. You can apply at over 5000 US government offices, including some post offices. If you want to speed up your application, you'll have to pay more for it. However, if you are at all tight for time, that might be your best course.

To apply for a passport you must prove that you are a genuine citizen by producing a previous passport or your birth, naturalization, or citizenship certificate. You have to complete a form, submit two passport photos and your social security number, and pay the application fee.

If you already have a passport, have you checked that it is still valid? Passports must be renewed every 10 years. I once was going to Morocco from Spain and my friend had not realized that her passport was due to expire in a few weeks. When we tried to check in, the airline staff were unwilling to let her on the plane. We persuaded them to let her board and when we got to our destination, we were able to arrange an extension on her passport. However, we achieved this only through a fluke, and we could have lost precious days of our trip. The moral of this story is that if you already have a valid passport, make sure it doesn't run out for six months from the date you're traveling. Check also that it's got enough blank pages to fit the visas you might need.

Visas

These are the pretty stamps in your passport that you need to visit certain countries. Find out if you need a visa to visit your destination. Learn where to get it, whether you can apply beforehand, or if it is better to get one on the border or on arrival. If you have to apply beforehand, how long will it take? Do you need a single or a multiple entry? Visas can be expensive—so how much does it cost?

Visa regulations change, so it's best to check this information with the embassy of your destination country than to make assumptions about it. But it's not as scary as it sounds. Embassies are very helpful. They will guide you through the process step by step and make it as simple as possible.

Discount cards

Investigate widely to find out what's available in the way of deals on discount cards that might be useful overseas—youth hostel cards, student cards, teacher cards, automobile club cards, senior citizen cards, or any others. You'll be surprised how often you can get into attractions or pay half price for transportation with plastic in your pocket.

2 Fearless
Taking-off

*"He who would travel happily
must travel light."*

SAINT-EXUPERY

The big day is approaching at last. Taking off can be the most exciting and nerve-racking time of any trip. This is the period when all the anticipation for your voyage of discovery mingles with the unknown factors that rattle around in the back of your mind—the niggling doubts or "What ifs." What if something unthinkable happens? What if I forget something vital? How will I cope with this trip?

Well, fear not. This chapter is about calming those natural jitters and building a fail-safe travel kit to cope with any situation that might arise. Most of the time, it's a huge relief to actually arrive and find out that things are far simpler than you thought they would be.

And to make things easier for you, we've added a packing checklist at the back of the book with plenty of useful stuff not mentioned here: *see* p.160. So all that remains is for you to start packing!

WHAT TO PACK

With a job as a roaming travel writer, I have to pack and unpack my bag on an almost constant basis. So I've come to appreciate the need for packing in an organized fashion to minimize fuss. But when it comes down to it, packing is a personal process and varies according to your destination and traveling style.

Travel light, travel happy

The lighter you travel, the more fancy-free you will be. A smaller suitcase or pack is not only easier carry around, it also frees you to travel in whatever fashion you like.

Size matters!

Choose the smallest or lightest items you can find. It's a great idea to hoard small plastic bottles for toiletries and replenish them when they run low. Aerosols can also be substituted by something smaller: look for special mini-bottles of shaving oil instead of shaving foam, a deodorant stick rather than a can. To save lots of space, use one of the lightweight travel towels now available. They dry quickly and take up almost no space.

Be versatile and improvise!

Always think versatility when you're packing. Making a few items go a long way will save space, energy and time. Sweaters make good travel pillows, and film canisters double as pill bottles, moisturizer tubs, or shot glasses.

Sarong: You can use it as a sheet, picnic blanket, towel, headscarf, neck scarf, curtain, or a "changing room" at the beach. Plus, you can gather it into a hobo-style bag or use it to lie on at the beach.

Bandanna: This can double as a hanky, headband, sleeping mask, scrubbing cloth, or bandage. Wrap it around your hand to prevent blisters during heavy work, or tie it around pressure points to stop blood flow in emergencies.

Plastic bags: It's the simplest things that are often the most important—and as proof, the humble plastic bag has multiple uses for the fearless traveler. If you're a backpacker, lining your bag with a trash bag stops your gear from getting soaked or dirty when you're on the move. You can also pack wet or muddy gear in plastic bags and keep bottles and cosmetics in a bag with a zipper closure to prevent ruining your clothes if a bottle should spill or break. Trash bags can be transformed into an effective jacket in a pinch, and during a storm in Thailand, the rain blew straight into our flimsy bamboo beach hut. The solution? Pin garbage bags to the inner wall!

Pocketknife: You can't take it in your hand luggage if you're flying, so pack it in the hold. This neat device does everything from opening beer bottles to cutting toenails. Look for a quality knife with a strong blade. Don't choose an inexpensive one with too many gizmos, as they tend to be more flimsy.

GIZMOS AND GADGETS

Imagination is a traveller's best friend, and creativity and endurance can substitute for fancy travel devices. But they're a great help if you can afford them. And there are plenty on the market: everything from the ubiquitous inflatable pillow for cat napping on public transportation to solar-powered mosquito repellents and sophisticated padlocks that recognize your fingerprint. Most are available from good camping stores, but for specialized items, check out the recommended websites.

Compass: Of course, a good ol' compass will do the job for most of us. Use a small one to help orientate yourself when emerging from subways or buses in cities.

Language translators: The size and shape of a calculator, these devices can store and translate numerous different languages and even show you how to say each phrase. Some devices have sound and will pronounce them for you. The snazzier versions also allow you to store business information, calculate money exchanges, and set an alarm to wake you up for that early flight. See http://www.ectaco.com.

Head Flashlight: These new super-light flashlights on a headband have recently come on the market, and they are pure joy to use. They keep your hands free and always point in the right direction.

GPS (Global Positioning System) Receivers:

Imagine you have no clue where you are—not hard for your average traveler. Forget landmarks, laboriously drafted maps, or reading the stars in the night sky. This pocket-sized gizmo tells you exactly where you are on Earth at any given moment. GPS is actually a constellation of Earth-orbiting satellites. The receiver locates these, figures out the distance to each, and uses this information to pinpoint its own location. It even gives altitude, so trekkers, skiers, and mountaineers can tell with absolute precision when they're up a mountain in the middle of nowhere. Get information from http://www.garmin.com/outdoor.

Travel lock: Padlocks are always useful, but a new and more versatile breed of travel lock is now available. These ingenious gadgets can lock almost any door, window, drawer, or cupboard—even if they don't have a latch. The device consists of two adjustable plates of metal that connect and wedge your door, closet, or drawer closed. You then immobilize the plates with a combination lock.

Universal drain plug: If you're going to countries in the developing world, it's worth taking a few extras. I've stayed in many hundreds of hotel rooms throughout the developing world, but I could probably count on one hand the ones that had plugs in the sink. That's why this little circular rubber gadget is a great help; use it to block any drain when filling the sink. It has different rubber rings to fit any size.

If the shoe fits . . .

Question: What are your most valuable travel accessories? **Answer:** Your feet! Take good care of them, pack comfortable walking shoes, and—believe me—you'll have a much happier vacation. Just don't take too many; shoes have a way of taking up far too much room. Aim to take two versatile pairs: one that supports and protects the foot, such as athletic shoes or hiking boots if you're a trekker, and a lighter pair such as a pair of sandals. Make doubly sure the sandals are comfortable, because if anything causes you grief, it will probably be the sandals.

Never ever take footwear that you have not already broken in unless you want to go through enough Band-Aids to patch up Humpty Dumpty. My favorite hiking boots took me six weeks of agony to soften enough to walk normally. To this day, I maintain that they broke me in, not the other way around!

If you really want to pamper tired, sore feet, take along some peppermint lotion and treat any sore spots with moleskin, corn pads, or Band-Aids. If you wear sandals, don't forget to put sun block on your feet or you'll get beautiful red stripes.

Dressing for anything

Deciding what clothes to take along is always one of the central concerns of the prepared traveler—and should depend almost entirely on the nature and destination of your trip. Wherever you're heading, you'll want to be dressed for the occasion. It's also important to respect local customs when deciding what to wear abroad. *See* Chapter 4, p 87.

Tropical climate

Whether you soak up the sun like a basking reptile or it makes you wilt like a flower in a desert, you'll need the right clothing to stay cool, comfortable, and healthy in hot tropical climates.

Think carefully about fabrics. Cotton and other natural fabrics are the coolest and allow your skin to breathe, although they crease easily. Cotton skirts are especially cool and comfortable because they allow air to circulate. Synthetics often dry more quickly, wrinkle less easily, but are hot and sticky. I never take jeans to hot countries because they're heat traps, take forever to dry, and weigh three times as much as cotton pants. In contrast, silk looks great, is cool in a hot climate and warm in a cool one, lightweight, and dries fast.

Loosely fitting clothes are also practical because they let air circulate. You can roll them up when you're at the beach, crossing rivers, or in flooded areas. Poorly drained areas of Calcutta get flooded almost knee-deep in monsoon downpours, but with my loose, cotton trousers rolled up, I could negotiate my way to dry land without looking ridiculous.

When traveling in monsoon-ridden tropical countries, I also take along a small, folding umbrella instead of a waterproof jacket. Numerous trips taught me that an anorak is stiflingly hot, whereas an umbrella lets you walk in a tropical downpour in comfort. In India, the local ladies often carry an umbrella—partly to shelter from the late monsoon squalls, but also to give shade from the scorching sun once the clouds cleared. Their kaleidoscopically colorful flowing saris topped off with brightly colored umbrella-sunshades make them look so extraordinarily elegant that, on my latest trip, I snapped a whole roll of camera film simply trying to capture them.

Wear long sleeves and pants to thwart mosquitoes. It's also a good idea to protect your head from the sun with a hat. If you're unsure about whether shorts are acceptable in the local culture, take pants with leg bottoms that zip off to make an instant pair of shorts.

Variable and moderate climates

Perhaps you're going on a trip to England during the spring, when you could enjoy glorious sunshine one minute and hailstones the next. Or maybe you're traveling to a country as varied as Chile, which not only has the world's driest desert, but also boasts some of the world's highest mountains and awe-inspiring glaciers. So how do you pack to prepare for all of these diverse weather conditions? And even more to the point, how can you do it without having a truck to carry all the necessary clothes around?

Clever combinations

The simple solution is to take clothing that is adaptable to each situation. While it's tempting to take thick jackets for a few days in the mountains, they take up a great deal of valuable packing space and will see little use throughout the rest of your journey. It's far better to think in terms of mixing and matching your other clothing, which in the right combinations can be as warm as any thick, bulky jacket.

The easiest way to stay warm, comfortable, and dry come rain, shine, warmth, or cold is to dress in a series of loose, lightweight layers. Layers create pockets of air that trap your body heat and keep you as snug as you need to be. And their great versatility gives you far more control over your temperature—simply add on or strip off layers as temperatures fluctuate. This is far more effective than the either-on-or-off extremes of a thick jacket.

You'll want an insulating layer such as thermal knits next to your skin. Today you can get great designs. The best "wick" sweat away from your skin and let it evaporate without robbing you of body heat. The next layer should be a good insulator, like a light, closely woven sweater or fleece. And finally, your outermost layer should be wind and rain proof. Mix and match as necessary and you'll be prepared for anything.

Cold climates

Of course, if you're going skiing, snowboarding, mountaineering, or whale-watching in the Antarctic, you won't want to skimp on warm clothing: it's vital to take a good selection of thermal knits, thick sweaters, fleeces, wool leggings, gloves, scarves, chunky socks, and a thick jacket—preferably made with down. Wearing layers is still a good strategy, especially for high-energy winter sports, but for low-activity trips in freezing conditions, that thick down jacket is vital.

On a trip cross-country skiing in Norway, my companions and I started the day by almost doubling our body weight by wrapping ourselves up in several layers of thermals, fleeces, thick pants, leggings, waterproofs, and socks. However, once we were skiing and working up a sweat, we rapidly shed layers. The only parts of our bodies that stubbornly refused to heat up with the exercise were our toes, which became painfully frozen despite all our layers. We ended up buying disposable, chemical toe-warmer pads now available in camping or skiing stores. Once the packaging is removed and they are exposed to the air, the chemical warmers kick into action. They can keep your toes toasty warm for up to five hours of freezing temperatures.

WHAT NOT TO TAKE

It's fun to stock up on new gear, gadgets, and clothes before your big trip. They will make you feel more prepared and increase your anticipation about getting on the road. But remember the travel-light mantra and try not to get too carried away when you're packing. If you bring everything, you'll need your own personal porters to drag your bags around!

Function versus weight

So how should you decide what not to take? Keeping your luggage down to size is no easy task, and you must make some hard decisions. Here's a strategy that works for me: For everything you want to pack, consider how much it weighs against how much it will be used. Can you justify that inflatable beach mattress or travel iron? If you're going on a short beach trip, then maybe you can. But if it's unlikely you'll use it frequently, consider leaving it behind or buying one when the need arises. Some backpackers take sleeping bags, tent, and stove despite camping infrequently. In many trekking regions it's easy to rent camping gear, and in others, such as Nepal, you can simply stay in remote villages that cater to trekkers. Similarly, a mosquito net is bulky and not always necessary. Try finding a hotel room with a mosquito net—they're common in places where the little pests are a problem.

A heavy read

Nothing weighs down your baggage like books. A couple of guidebooks and novels can weigh as much as all your clothes put together. Of course, you could discard or mail books home after reading them—an expensive option—or you could swap them as you go along. Plenty of travelers do this. Hotels often have a collection of books left behind by other travelers, and you can often swap with traveling friends too. It's a cheap, light, and easy way to broaden your reading horizons.

Another strategy used by some people is to buy inexpensive, used paperback books and rip out each chapter after reading it. This way, my friend was able to take along the complete *War and Peace* without having its weight drag her down.

MEDICINES, COSMETICS

As noted earlier, it's normal to try to protect yourself from unpleasant situations when traveling abroad, and this is especially true when it comes to health and happiness.

So it's natural to want to carry an entire medicine chest around on your back wherever you go. In my early traveling days, I took along enough emergency remedies to stock a small drugstore. However, unless you are very unlucky, you'll rarely use all of the medical supplies you take abroad—and as you travel more extensively, you'll probably start to trust your environment a little more. Drugstores and hospitals around the world are most familiar with ailments specific to their region, so their advice is often invaluable.

That said, some precautions are necessary to keep fearless travelers in fine shape. You certainly must take a first-aid kit, pain-killers, and precautions against insects, fungus, blisters, and the sun. Take along lip balm, motion sickness tablets, and a few anti-diarrhea drugs. Where appropriate, it's best to bring your own supply of malaria tablets, tampons, contraceptive pills, and condoms—plus copies of any prescriptions, just in case.

Looking good, feeling good

Even if you love to look your best in every situation, travel has a way of leaving beauty routines by the wayside. However, looking your best can boost your confidence and happiness in a new country. Try to do this without packing too much: Buy small packages or plastic bottles of your favorite products and use sample cosmetics from store promotions. Alternatively, buy small tubs and bottles from travel stores and fill them with your favorite products. Remember that liquids expand during flight, so leave enough space to allow for this.

Always put containers of liquid items in sealed plastic bags to avoid disasters. And put a small square of some plastic wrap over the bottle head before screwing on the lid. This tightens the lid and helps stop up any gaps. Lipstick messes are another hazard—hot climates melt lipsticks, so it's better to take lip pencils with you.

Water of life

Staying well-hydrated in foreign climes is common sense and vitally important for your travel health and happiness. So drink plenty of fluids when you're traveling. It's easy to lose track of just how much valuable water and salts you're losing while sweating in hot climates or suffering mild bouts of travel diarrhea. This is one of the most common causes of energy loss and lethargy when you're traveling, and it's a good idea to take precautions.

The simplest solution is dissolving some salt and sugar into drinking water. Drinking flat soft drinks can also help a bit. But if you can, take a few specially designed packets of flavored, soluble rehydration salts that are commonly available in pharmacies. They taste much better than dissolved salt and sugar alone and supply all the essential salts your body needs to function properly, so they restore your pep and help you put your best fearless foot forward.

On the subject of water, it's often best to avoid drinking tap water in foreign countries because it can contain impurities harmful to foreigners. Of course, you can usually get by on bottled mineral water. However, there are also several cunning ways to zap the nastiest microbes in tap water when necessary. You can buy tablets or small dropper bottles of purifying chemicals such as iodine or chlorine. Alternatively, you can choose from a range of water filters that pump water through a purifying system, though these are bulkier and more expensive than chemical purifiers.

Toilet humor

This may not be a suitable topic for dinner conversation, but every seasoned traveler has a story to tell about nasty toilet experiences in far-flung places. And whether its squat-style toilets in French camping sites, open-fronted street-side urinals in India, or a mosquito-infested open pit at a jungle camp, our revulsion at strange and often unhygienic toilet standards abroad does make a funny story that can shock or amuse folks back home.

Even if you're planning to stay in first class quality hotels with sparklingly clean bathrooms, you're still likely to find yourself having to use the local-style toilets at tourist attractions, in restaurants, and on trips into the countryside. So be prepared. This preamble brings me to what—in some countries—must be the most important travel tip of all.

Don't ever count on finding toilet paper in any toilet that you visit. Always, but always, carry your own.

Natural remedies

How about trying natural or local solutions to minor health niggles? For example, one of the best natural mosquito deterrents is eating lots of garlic. No kidding. They can't abide the smell. And it's an anti-fungal food rich in nutrients too. Just buy a pack of garlic tablets from your local pharmacy. Of course, you might want to watch your intake to prevent garlic breath from driving off more than the mosquitoes! On another note, one of the best treatments for minor burns is aloe vera.

This fleshy-leaved, spiny plant grows wild in the sub-tropical western hemisphere. Just slice open one of the leaves and smear the gloopy, yellowish, juice on sunburn to soothe the skin and encourage healing.

Homeopathic remedies can often help with common problems such as travel fatigue and motion sickness. Also, keep an ear to the ground for local remedies wherever you're going. For instance, in the high reaches of the Andes, a centuries-old treatment for altitude sickness is chewing on or making tea from the bitter-tasting coca leaf from which cocaine is made. Don't panic—the tea is perfectly legal.

TECHNIQUES FOR GOOD PACKING

The right bags

If you're planning to do a lot of traveling, you'll be spending lots of time hauling luggage around, so it's vitally important to get the right bag. Your preferred method of travel will, of course, play a big part in this decision.

If you're going on a short break or you like to pack light, a bag small enough to avoid having to check it on a plane can be a great advantage. You'll avoid the baggage-claim lines and also be certain that none of your luggage is misdirected to the other side of the world. For those who don't want to carry heavy bags, consider getting a bag with built-in wheels. Look for one that rolls smoothly, is easy to maneuver, and is lightweight, stable, and roomy.

Also consider height when you're choosing a case or bag. After all, shorter people don't want the handle height to be around their chest and tall people don't want to be reaching down to shin-height the whole time!

Backpackers should take particular care when choosing a pack. A really good travel pack becomes a familiar traveling buddy that accompanies you though amazing journeys. I've taken mine on many dozens of trips and now feel heartbroken at the thought of buying a new one. A good backpack should sit snugly against your back and distribute the weight to prevent back strains. Heavy-duty external frame packs are good for trekking but are awkward for everyday travel, while soft packs are more maneuverable. If you expect to splurge on souvenirs at the end of your trip, consider one of the "expandable" backpacks that can be adjusted to create more space when needed.

Also pack at least one daypack. You're bound to use it for shopping, hiking, and other excursions. Look for a bag made of lightweight material so that it can pack down super-small.

Fearless baggage security

It's always a good idea to personalize your bag to prevent mix-ups in the baggage claim. Buy any color other than black, because that's the most common choice, and wrap brightly colored ribbon or tape around it. And if you're feeling artistic, there's no need to stop there—go wild with a paint box if the mood takes you. I once saw a proud parent's suitcase decked out in psychedelic handprints that had been painted by their toddler; there was no way that this family's bag was going to get mistaken for anybody else's.

If you're worried about security, don't use the pickable little padlocks that come with suitcases; buy your own. And if you use a pack with only a drawstring at the top, pass a light chain through the top and padlock it. It may not stop a serious thief, but it's a decent deterrent for some opportunists. For example, bags often ride on top of buses in South America, and it's also common for some passengers to hop on the roof when the bus is full. Rooftop riders could amuse themselves by rifling through backpacks.

Use luggage ID tags, but don't write your home address on them. You don't want to advertize that your house is empty in case someone is noting such things. Instead, use your business address and phone.

Packing systems

Every fearless traveler will have his or her own system for packing. Some people claim that rolling their clothes saves space and prevents creases. Others swear that "bundling" clothes tightly around a large central object is the best way to prevent all creasing and wrinkling. The latter method is great if you're going on a business trip and you really have to be crisp and wrinkle-free when you get there.

To do this, pile up your clothing on a flat surface such as a bed, smoothing out each piece as you go. Start with the largest pieces first, building up to the smaller ones on top. Lay each item in alternate directions to keep an even thickness. When all the pieces of clothing are piled up, put a large core item, such as your rolled up washbag, on top of them, then wrap each piece firmly around it one by one. You then fit the resulting bundle tightly into your bag, and *voila*! Pristine and wrinkle-free clothing on arrival.

Alternatively, you could try simply folding clothes together. Take two items of clothing and lay them out, one half covering the other. Then fold the bottom item over the top layer where they overlap. Repeat this with the free half of the top layer so that they each cushion each other from creases.

A few travel wrinkles are par for the course. A good way to get rid of them is to hang your clothes in a steamy bathroom when you arrive—the steam relaxes the creases so you can step out fearless and flawless later on.

Space-saving techniques

For many people, packing to leave on a trip is not a big problem. But squeezing everything back in your case after a holiday shopping spree can be another matter. Try to make every inch count. Stuff all the empty spaces—such as inside your shoes or the hollow in a cup—with small items like underwear. Wedge small towels into cracks around other items. Pack shoes tightly together, soles out, with the heels at opposite ends. Stand your closed case or backpack up and drop it to the floor a couple of times. The contents should settle enough to create more space.

> *Some short-term travelers also take specially made, airtight plastic bags from travel stores to help fit everything back into their suitcase. By rolling these transparent bags tightly, you squeeze all the excess air from fabrics then seal them shut, creating a surprising amount of extra space. But remember, it might save room but won't save weight; think twice about buying that fifth yak-wool sweater if you're carrying your own luggage.*

Clutter busters

There are hundreds of travel organizers on the market these days: multi-compartmented bags, pouches, totes, and anything that a jet-setting wanderer may want to keep their bits and pieces in. If you're as disorganized as I am, these bags can be a tremendous help keeping your loot in order. I often send up a little prayer of thanks to the person who designed my lightweight wash bag, which folds out into several sections with see-through mesh pockets, and has a hook on top so I can hang it for easy access. This is a fantastic alternative to unpacking toiletries in every hotel bathroom. Just unzip, hang up, and everything's within grasp. It's got superb space management, too. I've been in many a budget hotel's bathroom that's so small you have to sit on the toilet to take a shower. No chance of spreading out toiletries there!

Buddy up

Traveling with a partner or fearless friend gives you a terrific advantage for packing when you want to keep the weight down. You can share things such as medical supplies, heavy guidebooks, and a dozen other little bits. That's a big weight off your mind—and your back.

Airline restrictions

There's no getting away from it: airline rules are getting stricter all the time. You have to keep an eye on weight and size restrictions, but the changes also mean you'll have to be doubly careful of what you pack in your carry-on luggage. Airline regulations now prohibit carrying on anything with blades, and yes, that includes a nail file, corkscrew, penknife, and the mini sewing scissors you got in a Christmas stocking. Airlines just can't take any chances, however innocent these things may seem. So always pack such items into checked luggage or you'll lose them.

TIPS FOR AIR TRAVEL

Now that you're packed and raring to go, it's getting to be time for take-off. The following tips make your flight a more relaxing experience. So why not try them out so you can relax and look forward to your trip with pleasure.

 ## Fearless flying

Some people never quite get used to the sensation of flying in an airplane. A fear of heights, claustrophobia, or anxiety about losing control usually underpins such worries. It's a common problem, and even frequent flyers sometimes get jangling nerves. My traveling companion Harry has been unnerved by flying all his life and clings so hard to my arm during take-off that he practically stops the circulation. But despite this fear, he has managed trips all around the world and doesn't regret them for an instant. There are no miracle cures, but a useful tip he gives is to keep a close eye on the flight attendants. If they look calm during the plane's bumps and wobbles, you can be sure you're safe.

Furthermore, don't drink caffeinated drinks before or during the flight. They can exacerbate anxiety. It's also a good idea to distract yourself as much as possible. Take games and books and talk to the person next to you. Before your trip, learn some relaxation techniques such as deep breathing or meditation. And visualize yourself already at your destination and having a wonderful time. Some people also take a mild sedative or an aspirin to help settle their jitters.

Don't be timid about asking your doctor or a therapist for advice if you're seriously worried about flying. For some people, just talking about the problem can help.

Stretch yourself

My nickname of "dusty-butt" perhaps explains why I smile when discussing the limited amount of legroom on planes. Being short can be a distinct advantage for travelers. But I've traveled with enough long-legged people to know the real misery caused by a lack of legroom on long flights.

Asking for the aisle seat won't help; you can't stick your legs into the aisles because the flight attendants need it for beverage and food carts and other travelers use it to get to the restrooms. So here's the trick: arrive early and ask for bulkhead seats or a window seat near an emergency exit. These spots always have plenty of legroom. Bulkhead seats are also good for traveling with kids because there's more room to stand without going into the aisle. If you want to make doubly sure, ask for seat assignments when you make the flight reservation. This way, you can stretch out without fear of making the flight attendants trip and deposit the evening meal all over you.

Vulnerable veins

Also known as the "Economy Class Syndrome," Deep Vein Thrombosis (DVT) has been a hot topic on the news in recent years. So what is it, and how can you prevent it? Well, DVT refers to blood clots that can form in veins. If a large clot fragments and travels around the body, it can obstruct the blood flow to important areas. In susceptible people, inactivity, low oxygen pressure, and the dry air that's common in planes can trigger these problems. It sounds scary, but don't let this worry you too much.

The good news is that taking a few simple precautions can help to prevent DVT. Moving your legs regularly and drinking plenty of water both help. You could also wear compression socks; these specially designed garments compress the foot and lower leg, helping circulation.

Popping ears

As for the hiccups, there are dozens of popular cures to help stop your ears from popping. Solutions range from sucking on hard candies to putting two cups over your ears to equalize the pressure! Some people swear by sipping drinks, swallowing, yawning, or using earplugs. Experiment and find what works best for you.

What a carry on

It's best to take valuables, a change of clothes, and your toothbrush in your hand luggage—just in case your checked luggage has another route in mind. Although lost luggage is an infrequent occurrence, it can still happen from time to time. If you get caught in a situation like that, you'll be glad you carried on that fresh set of undies.

Keep on moving

Ever stepped off a plane feeling akin to the zombies in *Night of the Living Dead*? Why not try a few simple exercises to prevent your muscles from stiffening up because you sat still for too long a period? Remember to rotate your shoulders and bend your neck to each side and back and forth a couple of times every hour—this makes you feel far more relaxed. You should stretch your arms and legs when possible, too, and get up and walk around whenever you get the chance. It's really important to keep that blood flowing.

Restful flight

The first things to go in my carry-on airplane bag are always the most important—earplugs! You may not look the height of cool with psychedelic-colored, plastic blobs sticking out of your ears, but you'll look far worse if that bawling baby in the next row keeps you awake for a 20-hour journey. So plug them in, sit back, and enjoy a far less stressful flight.

Minimizing jet lag

We all suffer from tiredness and disorientation after rapidly crossing several time zones. It's a natural disruption of our daily routines. Suddenly you're itching to go for a jog at

3:00 a.m. or wanting to stay in bed until the stars come out. Although there's no way to avoid jet lag completely, you can help your body adjust to its new time zone more smoothly. Follow these steps and you'll be able to start your fearless travels rested and with a clear head.

1. **Go to bed early for several days before your trip.**
2. **Catch as much shut-eye as you can during the flight.**
3. **Avoid flight dehydration, because it exacerbates jet lag. Drink lots of water and avoid caffeinated drinks and alcohol.**
4. **Be sure to drink lots of water after your flight, too. It flushes out your system and helps you feel less sluggish.**
5. **Spend lots of time outside in the daylight when you arrive and your body will naturally start readjusting its internal clock.**
6. **Take it easy when you arrive! Relax into the local time slowly, but try not to collapse into bed until the evening. That helps you to adjust more quickly.**

OTHER MODES OF TRANSPORT

Of course, not all of us will be jumping on a plane to reach our chosen destination. Plenty more people are opting for less expensive, more convenient, or even more luxurious options. If you feel up to it, mixing and matching your methods of transport often lets you get the most fun and action out of your trip.

Fearless cruises

This is the life! Traveling by cruise ship can be one of the most luxurious, relaxing, and romantic methods of getting around. You can move around the world without ever leaving your five-star comforts behind. It's a safe and comfortable way to first venture out into the world, and the only real worries you'll have to combat are seasickness, eating too much, and potential boredom. More and more Americans are signing up to travel on increasingly affordable cruise ships.

Know your ship: Remember you're going to be tied to your cruise ship once it's left the harbor, so it's worth making doubly sure it's the right ship for you beforehand. Of course its itinerary is important, but equally, you should think about the ship itself. Who are the typical customers—young, old, single, or honeymooners? Are kids welcome? If so, are there enough entertainment options to keep them amused? Does it have much nightlife? Ask as many questions as possible to make sure you're picking the right boat.

How adventurous do you want to be? If traveling abroad worries you, taking a cruise ship can be a great compromise. But just because you're taking a cruise doesn't mean you can't have an adventurous trip to places other vacationers can't easily reach. After all, you can't backpack your way around Antarctica with ease—a cruise is the way to go. On most cruises, there are flexible degrees of adventure. To avoid getting cabin fever, sign up for a cruise with as many shore excursions as possible. As you become more confident, you may also want to organize some more adventurous independent shore excursions. They are less expensive and often yield a lot more fun and excitement.

Queasy stomachs: If you get seasick simply at the thought of a stormy sea, don't rely on calm waters and the occasional motion-sickness tablet. You don't want your dream cruise ruined by a stomach as rough as the sea. It helps to put some thought into which boat and cabin position you'd like. Remember that the bigger the boat, the less rolling and seasickness it induces. Another tip is to try to secure a cabin in the middle of the boat, because the boat's center of gravity experiences the least movement.

Avoiding the bus blues

What you expect from bus travel at home may not prepare you for buses in other parts of the world. Outside North America, buses can be one of the least comfortable forms of long-distance transportation. Not only do they travel on roads that are not well maintained, they are frequently overcrowded. You should not be surprised to find a strange toddler on your lap or some unfortunate chickens en route to the market under your seat. But don't let that put you off.

Traveling by bus can be a terrific adventure and can provide lots of opportunities for valuable cultural insights. There's nothing like a bus ride for getting a really close up view of how local people live. You can simply sit back and enjoy the scenery without the fuss of driving or checking into airports.

Many countries do have efficient, commodious bus services, so bus travel doesn't always have to be a trauma for those who like their creature comforts. In any case, because traveling by bus is one of the cheapest ways to go, the enormous savings you make will often outweigh any passing discomfort.

Protein boosts: Interminable bus and train journeys can sometimes make eating well a tough proposition. Stations usually sell energy and junk food, but this carbohydrate-rich diet can leave you feeling undernourished. Tuck a can of tuna and can opener, a small jar of peanut butter or savory spread, or a few small, wax-covered cheeses into your pack. I was once forced to spend a night curled up in a cold and rickety old chicken bus in the Andes because rain had washed out the road. In the morning, I could not have been happier about my store of travel nibbles.

Make yourself comfortable: Bring whatever you need to feel at ease, because you're likely to be stuck in one place for a long time. Earplugs, travel pillows, and secure money belts give peace of mind if you doze off. I once woke up on a night bus taking the long and winding road into the high Andes to find a shadowy figure reaching into my pocket, obviously tempted by the wide rectangular shape bulging there. Unluckily for the figure, who made a fast exit from the bus, the rectangular shape was merely a small, flattened roll of toilet paper. All my money was safely tucked into a money belt under my clothes.

Bathroom breaks: I'll take the risk of sounding like your mother by loudly reminding you that you'll never regret going to the toilet before boarding long-distance buses, even if you don't feel the need to go right then. In many countries, it's extremely rare for buses or coaches to have on-board toilets, and bathroom stops on the road can be very erratic. I once sat out a non-stop, eight-hour bus journey in Bolivia with no toilet on board, and to this day I am in awe of the iron strength of the Bolivian bladder.

Seat choice: Sitting in the back or directly over the wheels can make for a bumpier bus ride than you bargained for, especially in developing countries where the roads are unpaved or badly potholed. So wherever possible, make sure you avoid these seats, especially on overnight journeys. One of my worst bus journeys was an overnight trip in northern India along shockingly bad roads. We bought the tickets at the very last minute and were left with the back row; our legs were immobilized when the people in front of us put back their seats. But at least having our knees painfully pinned down stopped our heads from hitting the ceiling of the bus each time the driver hit a pothole, which he seemed to do roughly every few seconds.

Daytime travel: While we're on the subject of overnight travel, if you're traveling in a region famous for its scenery—don't waste your trip. Take buses during the daylight so you can watch the land and towns speed past your window.

Discounts: Before setting off, check whether there are any discount cards for your route. In many countries, you can buy a bus pass that allows you to travel around for a month or so, stopping when you feel like it. For example, Ameripass and other Greyhound Discovery Passes are good in the USA and Canada, Busabout gives discounts in Europe, and Baz Bus (www.bazbus.com) works in South Africa. Research this in advance and you may save a packet.

Fearless road trip

For many of us, the summer vacation heralds long road trips with loved ones or friends. It's an especially good way for families to travel. As a child, I loved sitting and watching cities, towns, farmlands, rivers, and mountains roll past on our trips throughout Europe. As an adult, the road trip also came to symbolize getting away from it all—hitting the open road with, or without, your loved ones and driving off into the sunset.

Best wheel forward: Of course, a fearless road trip starts with good preparation. In particular, make certain that your lights, signals, wiper blades, horn, and spare tire are in good shape. You should also check fluid levels, tire pressure, belts, caps, hoses, and filters. You don't want breakdowns or necessary mechanical work eating into your big adventure. On the same theme, remember to pack an emergency road kit with useful tools and spares.

Scenic route: The great thing about road trips is the control you have over your own destiny, so make the most of it. Take scenic drives and turn-offs whenever you feel like it. Detour off the freeways and explore the back roads. This gives you an entirely different, and usually rewarding view of a region

Rental-car discounts: There are so many discounts and deals available in the competitive world of rental cars that you almost never have to accept standard rates. Book your rental car early and shop around on the Internet. Check your guidebook for cheaper national companies—as opposed to the international big guns—in your chosen destination. Call your credit card banks and frequent flyers programs to ask about special discounts. And if you're flying, ask the airline if they have special offers with rental car companies. Once you've found a deal you like, read the fine print. Ask about any local surcharges, taxes, insurance costs, and how much it costs to drop off your car at a different destination.

Rental-car checks: Once you've been shown to your rental car, check it for any damage or problems. If you spot anything, report it to the attendants immediately and ask them to sign and make a note of it on your rental paperwork. If you don't do this, you might end up getting charged for damage that somebody else did.

Fearless rail travel

Traveling by train has a certain timeless appeal for the restless, the romantic, and, of course, the roaming traveler. It's a very relaxing way to travel because you can just sit back and enjoy the ride. It's also a great way to travel with fidgety kids, because they don't have to stay put for long periods as they do in buses, and there's always something interesting to see in the passing landscape.

Don't waste the time: The great thing about using public transportation in foreign countries is that the journey is a cultural experience in itself. It gives you the opportunity to chat with the locals, who'll usually be just as curious about you as you are about them and also just as happy for some kind of distraction to make the trip go faster.

Discounts: In many countries, you can save a bundle of cash by signing up for a rail pass. For example, in Canada there's the Canrailpass; in Europe, the EurailPasses; and non-citizens visiting the USA can also get the USA Railpass. Think carefully about your itinerary before committing yourself to a pass, and always read the fine print. Not all trains are covered. You can also sometimes score discounts by mentioning your age, whether or not you are a student, or citing affiliations such as the AAA or AARP.

Get top bunks: You'll need to think a little about security on sleeper trains in some countries. For example, sleeper cars in India are almost always open with only a curtain if you're in higher classes. Because of that, it's safer to take the higher bunk and sleep with your head on your baggage.

Tips for amusing kids on long trips

Remember those interminable car journeys when you were stuck in the back seat? We all know the tedium that long journeys can inspire, and we all know that kids are the most easily bored creatures on earth. I remember long road trips with my young cousin singing the delightful little ditty "I know a song that gets on everybody's nerves," sung to the tune of *Battle Hymn of the Republic* and repeated at great length. There's no better recipe for vacation insanity!

Generations of frazzled parents have evolved their own tricks and ploys to prevent kids from making mischief on trips. Here are a few time-honored ideas.

1. Make your kids feel involved: show them your map and let them "direct" you by map reading and looking for signs.

2. A little bribery goes a long way. Pack a bag of surprises; toys, snacks, puzzles, magazines, games or anything that might be distracting. Make it a rule that if they don't argue or fight, they will get regular prizes.

3. Pack healthy but sweet snacks and drinks: fruits, raisins, and muesli bars are good choices. Try to avoid candies though. The fewer sugar-fueled energy-bursts they have, the smoother your journey will be.

4. On road trips, plan to stop frequently and let the kids run around so that they can release all that pent-up energy.

5. Listening to talking books is another great way to distract their minds and stop them from getting restless.

3 Fearless Touchdown

"...there was still room to turn around in, but not to swing a cat in, at least with entire security to the cat."

MARK TWAIN (on being shown to his room.)

On one of my first trips around Asia, I was a teenager, still wet behind the ears. This was the landmark trip on which I discovered the true value of being prepared for the culture shock of touchdown. Our flight to Mumbai was delayed, so we arrived at night. The 25-hour broken journey had left us shattered and we couldn't wait to reach a hotel room and a soft bed. After the ordeal of going through an interminable customs line, negotiating the money exchange, and finding our bags, we headed out into the damp, humid night to face a new country...

Shock! Up came the airport welcoming committee. An army of hard-sell hotel touts and taxi drivers instantly crowded about us—shouting, barging, gesticulating, and waving photos in our faces. We were too hot, tired, lost, and frazzled from our flight to fight our way through the crowd, and eventually caved in to their promises of clean sheets and hot showers. But the hotel they took us to was an overpriced, rat-infested pit with a leaking roof, in which we were disturbed every 10 minutes by a scowling bellboy demanding a larger tip. And after a restless, jet-lagged night plagued by mosquitoes and bedbugs, we discovered we were miles from where we had planned to stay. It was hardly the perfect start to our perfect trip!

Although I now look back on this experience and shudder, it taught me valuable lessons early on in my travels. The following tips were learned the hard way. They will help you leave the airport without problems and install yourself in the perfect place to stay—giving you a firm foothold and confident, fearless start. If only I had known them when I was that unworldly teenager...

TOUCHDOWN

So you've touched down and are blearily stumbling out into the daylight to come face to face with a whole new culture. It can be a shock to the system to deal with an onslaught of newness when you're not at your most alert. To some degree, this can't be avoided, but it can certainly be minimized with a little forethought.

Plan your arrival time

Start your trip the way you mean to go on—relaxed. It sets the tone for a stress-free trip if you plan your arrival and have a rough idea of what to expect. For one thing, it eases your blood-pressure levels if you can avoid arriving at night. Transportation from the airport is usually more straightforward in the daylight. And when the final buses or trains have left, the cabbies will almost certainly start charging vastly higher rates. I was once stuck at a taxi stand at 4:00 a.m. arguing with cabbies who were trying to charge $35 for a journey that should have cost a fifth of that! I ended up staying in the airport cafe until the morning, when taxi rates miraculously dipped once again. I took the bus anyway, as a protest.

Read the guidebook

Given my own experience writing travel guides, it's not surprising that I recommend religiously reading your guide-book's arrivals or airport section before touchdown. But it's valuable advice, anyway. Any guidebook worth its salt will put a tremendous amount of research into this section, knowing full well that newly arrived tourists are at their most disoriented and vulnerable. As such, it's reassuring to read exactly what to expect, and what to avoid, in your country of choice.

Lost luggage?

It's unlikely your luggage will be damaged or lost during the flight, but if something does happen, report it to the airport baggage staff immediately and fill out all the appropriate forms. Most airlines will give significant compensation, even if the bag turns up within a day. So get written confirmation of what's been lost and write down the name of the person who handled the report in case you need it later. Almost always, problems with straying bags will be smoothly and quickly resolved.

 ## Making a quick exit

Once you've arrived, you're likely to wonder if there is any way to speed up the interminable checks and re-checks at the airport. Each of the following strategies often helps:

1. If you look presentable, customs generally goes more quickly and smoothly. It's an unwritten law for many customs officials: the more tired and disheveled you look, the shiftier you seem. So brush your hair, shave if you're a man, and straighten those clothes.

2. If you followed the "travel light" section in Chapter 2, your bag might be so small that you didn't have to check it. This means that you don't have to wait for the luggage to be unloaded and can skip to the front of the customs line.

3. If you had to check your bags, try this one: at the counter, ask that your bags be classified as fragile. This means they should be placed at the top of the pile. With a bit of luck, they'll be among the first to appear in the luggage claim!

4. If you've reserved a rental car, you can save time by splitting tasks between traveling companions. One of you

can wait for the baggage while the other goes straight through customs to the rental desk, picks up the car, and returns to pick up everybody else at the arrival gate—ready and raring to go!

Transportation from the airport

Negotiating for a taxi can be a speedy affair in some countries, but in others it involves protracted wrangling. Taxi drivers will often try to overcharge you if they think you're not accustomed to the currency or appropriate rates. Always ask about typical prices at the information desk in the airport concourse. They will give you an honest estimate of what you should pay so you can avoid being fooled.

A flock of cab drivers usually swarms around you when you exit the airport. A cunning way to circumvent this is to zip around to the departures terminal and look for taxis that have just dropped off passengers. They're usually very happy to get a fare so quickly and often charge the best rates as a result.

However, for a fraction of the price of any taxi, take advantage of any available airport transfer services. Most big airports have a system of buses or vans that travel back and forth from the airport—often right to the doorstep of your chosen hotel. It's a cheap, easy, and stress-free solution.

Ask a hotel to pick you up

Many middle-range and top-end hotels offer a reasonably priced airport transfer service. This can make life far simpler. But always check the credentials of the driver who comes to pick you up. It sounds incredible, but I've seen more than a few cab drivers copy names of other drivers on to "welcome boards" to try and steal their customers.

PLACES TO STAY

Once you're safely out of the airport, you'll need to get yourself to a good place to stay, find your bearings, and recharge your batteries. And where you stay is of pivotal importance. If you're going to be traveling for a while, you'll be spending time and money finding and staying in various lodgings, so it's worth doing it well. Try these suggestions for discovering the perfect resting places.

The first night's stay

Indelible impressions of a country are often made during that crucial first night's stay. So even if you're a carefree creature of impulse, know that it's really important to book a place in advance to stay for your first night. You won't regret it. This is especially true if you've made a long trip. You're bound to be tired and a little lost in a new country, as I was when I got to Mumbai (*see* p. 65.) Having that first night hotel reservation is like putting a foot firmly in the door; you'll be aiming for a fixed and reliable point. So make sure that you always book a hotel that was recommended by a guidebook or other travelers and stick to your booking. The best assurance about the quality of a hotel or other lodging place always comes from people who have recently stayed there. They will tell you—honestly and in detail—exactly what to expect. However, if you don't have that resource, an independent, up-to-date guidebook makes a great backup.

Try to get a guide with long descriptions of hotels as they are likely to have taken the time and effort to make a close evaluation of the options. It's nice to be sure the researchers have actually been there, checked the hot-water faucets, talked to the staff, and soaked up the atmosphere. This sort of guide lets you know whether or not a particular hotel will suit your needs.

If you're booking hotels based on recommendations in a guidebook, make sure the guidebook you're using is a good choice. Some guides give only minuscule descriptions of accommodations—summing up a hotel's environment, position, amenities, and pros and cons in just four or five words.

BOOKING METHODS

So how should you go about booking your hotel? Do you want to do it over the phone, through a travel agent, or online? Not surprisingly, there are good arguments for each method.

Internet: You can often pick up good deals if you shop around and book online. Big hotel chains sometimes offer web-only deals. And you can browse photos, profiles, customer comments, and other indicators of how happy you'll be with a choice. However, don't accept everything they say. I've lost count of the number of far-flung hotels claiming to be a 20-minute ride from the airport. If you book your room online, don't forget to print the confirmation page and bring it along. It's also a good idea to confirm over the phone.

Check prices on a few websites—rates can vary according to who is touting them. Try the hotel's own website if it has one, as well as other reservations services. You could even try bidding for your chosen room on sites like Priceline or Hotwire: this can give you a lot more bang for your buck. I've known people who saved almost half the asking price this way.

Travel agents: Travel agents can make things smoother for you, even though impressive sounding savings can be swallowed up into their fees. They will generally confirm your room and usually help if things go wrong. If you have a good one, relax and let him or her do all the hard work.

Telephoning: This is my preferred method of booking lodging whenever I have a language in common with the staff. By contacting the hotel itself, you can be sure that the information you get will be reasonably accurate. After all, hotel staff know the rooms and facilities best. They may also quote better prices if you catch them at the right moment.

Making reservations in foreign languages

If you don't have a bilingual friend to help you out, try sending an e-mail. It gives the recipient time to decipher your message. Try copying and pasting your English e-mail text into an Internet translator site and paste the translated text to the bottom of the e-mail. Don't send just the translated copy because they are never 100% perfect. It's best to include your original along with the translation as it could help the recipient figure out what you were trying to communicate.

Reconfirm

No matter how you make your booking, remember that it's not necessarily final. Hotel owners are out to make a profit, and if they suspect a person is late or unreliable, they may not hold the room. Some hotels deliberately overbook to ensure a full house. So it's a good idea to call a second time shortly before your arrival. This is especially important if you're going to arrive later than planned. I once arrived at my Madrid hotel just 20 minutes later than arranged and found that they had given my room to somebody else 10 minutes earlier!

Beating budget blues

When you're newly arrived, tired, and jet-lagged, it's easy to start feeling down—especially if you're a budget traveler shacking up in a cheap hotel. It may cost just $2 a night, but you'll be happier if you've come prepared for basic conditions.

Maybe the sheets aren't pristine, or the pillow is yellow from years of use. Perhaps you're worried about security, noise, bedbugs, and other insects. I tend to treat myself to a mid-range hotel on my first night and move to cheaper accommodation afterwards, but every cent counts for some travelers. In these situations, you can take a few simple steps to ensure a more comfortable, restful start to your travels.

Take your own pillowcase and use your towel or sarong rather than the hotel sheets. And if you are unlucky enough to discover that there are bedbugs, spread a rain jacket or poncho onto the bed as a barrier first and lay your improvised sheet over that.

I often carry a little "luxury item" when I'm visiting developing countries with run-down budget hotels. It's a silk sleeping sheet that packs into a light bag the size of a hamburger bun. I bought it in a camping store and pull it out whenever I feel uncomfortable about a hotel's stained and cigarette-burned sheets. The silk also feels wonderful to snuggle up in, so I relax more quickly into a deep sleep. Also see the following pages for tips on security and noise-blockers to ensure your valuable beauty sleep. Trust me, everything looks completely different after a good night's sleep.

Know what you want

To find the perfect place to stay, it helps to know exactly what you want from it. Do some soul searching and decide what matters most to you on your dream trip. Location is vital, of course. Do you want a calm, de-stressing time in the country, relaxation and solitude on a castaway-style desert island, or a fabulous location on the brink of city nightlife?

The size and type of clientele at a hotel is also important. Would you rather have a friendly, personal service or do you feel happier to travel with anonymity? Do business folk, budget travelers, locals, or families generally stay at the hotel?

Are you hankering after luxury or bare-bones thriftiness? Does it really matter to you if the hotel has all the modern conveniences and amenities? If there's a pool or spa that you won't have time to take advantage of, then why pay for it?

Of course, what you want will sometimes change during the course of a trip. At the end of a marathon trip around Latin America, I shelled out for a hotel with plentiful hot water—a real luxury in budget hostels there. There had been times in the jungle when the only way to get myself truly clean was to stand out in a tropical rainstorm in a bikini with soap at the ready. And after trekking mountain trails, clinging on to the back of dirty trucks bouncing along dusty roads, sleeping in ancient, mildewed beds, and wielding machetes in sweaty jungle bush, a hot shower was something akin to heaven!

Once you've got an idea of what your dream lodging would be like, make it a reality. Check guidebooks and ask friends and traveling companions for recommendations. Phone hotels for information and don't be shy about asking awkward questions. If you have any preferences about location, view, bed size, room size, non-smoking rooms, or anything else, just ask.

Look around for your perfect spot

Once you've got your feet on the ground, it's easy to set about finding the right place. Imagine you're writing a mini-guidebook. Set yourself the tasks of asking people for recommendations, walking into hotels, and asking to see the rooms and facilities. Check that everything works. Try out the faucets and lights. Bounce on the bed to check its springiness. If there's a pool, check its size and that it's clean. Every hotel, hostel, or lodging that takes guests is used to this kind of questioning, so don't hold back. Be polite but ask them anything you want to know, even how they serve their toast in the morning if it's important to you. If they are unwilling to answer your questions, you know to move on to the next place.

Noisy neighborhoods

It can be a traveler's worst nightmare: You discover upon arrival that your handpicked hotel sits directly above a thumping nightclub or traffic roundabout that rings to the music of constant horns, screeching tires, and revving engines. Instead of tossing and turning sleeplessly, take some steps to block out the noise. Earplugs are the obvious solution to this problem, and I never travel without them. But how about creating white noise as a back-up solution? Tune the TV so that it creates nothing but static, or put on your portable radio and do likewise. The white noise will block out other, more disturbing noises such as rattles, creaks, bangs, and blaring horns, and help you sleep like a baby. Try it—it really works!

Variety is the spice of life

Mix and match your accommodations to see plenty of different sides of the place you're visiting. Be sure to work in a few small locally owned B&Bs and guesthouses if you can. These are the best places to have more contact with your hosts and the local culture. They are often the friendliest places, too. You're sure to get personalized service with all the local tips and gossip to boot.

In one homely Welsh B&B, we ended up befriending the owners and were subsequently treated like part of the family. We were invited to a laidback beach barbecue that developed into a night on the town visiting all the hottest new clubs that had not yet been listed in any guidebooks.

Booking ahead on the road

A common question from people traveling abroad for the first time is whether or not they should make an advance reservation for their accommodation. It certainly helps to avoid nasty surprises to book in advance for your first night or two. However, beyond this point, the answer lies where you're going, the kind of traveling you're doing, and the time of year.

For example, hotels in popular European capitals often fill up early during the summer and holidays, so it's always wise to reserve well in advance. However, if you're traveling independently in the tourist off-season, it's wiser to allow some flexibility in your itinerary and lodgings. You'll have a far more relaxed trip if your itinerary is not written in stone, and you can change hotels if you don't like the one where you're staying.

When you decide to make advance reservations, do your homework thoroughly to make sure you're not committing yourself to a room or hotel you wouldn't normally want to be in for even five minutes. Ask which are the best rooms, how big/light/noisy they are, if non-smoking rooms are available, if you can have one that faces away from the street, and if there is private parking. But if you haven't reserved a spot for the night, start looking around 3:00 or 4:00 in the afternoon. Hotels tend to fill up after this time.

Mixing in special places

Treating yourself to a really special hotel room every once in a while works wonders for your fearless state of mind. If you're on a tight budget, it can be an adventure to stay in the cheapest accommodations and live without any pampering. But the novelty can wear off. Remember, you're on vacation and should be relaxing, not punishing yourself, so refresh your batteries every once in a while by splurging on a nice hotel.

If you're traveling on a generous budget, schedule one or two really special locations—maybe an Irish castle-turned-hotel, a French château, Swedish ice-hotel, or a spa hotel—and let them treat you like royalty. You won't be sorry.

Every country has quirky accommodation options to tempt adventurous travelers, whether it's picturesque Thai river huts on stilts, remote farm haçiendas in the wilds of the Andes, centuries-old convents or monasteries in Portugal, Finnish igloo-hotels, a Czech converted prison, or an Indonesian longhouse. The possibilities are endless.

Luxury weekend breaks

Plenty of upper-crust city hotels suffer on the weekends when their business clients head home. Because of this, you can often find business hotels that will offer lower prices over the weekend, allowing you to live in the lap of luxury without breaking the bank. Conversely, in the countryside or by the beach, prices may go up on the weekends, but you'll get fantastic prices in the middle of the week.

Peace of mind

Some people would say that the most important thing a hotel can offer is safety. This is usually no problem in expensive hotels, but budget haunts can't usually afford to fork out on fancy alarm systems, or video surveillance. To choose reasonably secure lodgings, make a mental checklist of safety features. Always inspect the room before agreeing to take it. Are the door, windows, and locks sturdy and secure? Ask if access to the hotel is limited to guests-only, especially at night. If possible, look for a hotel with 24-hour security guards.

These things aren't always possible in budget hotels, but don't worry. You can take extra measures. For one, use your own padlock on the door. Good-sized, well-made combination locks are the best, because they have no keys to lose or carry while you're swimming or hiking. Alternatively, you could invest in a more versatile travel lock (*see* p. 32.)

Consider leaving your valuables in the hotel safe. Make a note of what you've left and don't leave anything too tempting. Take your money pouch with you when you go to the shower and either wear it or put it inside the pillowcase when you go to bed. That way you can relax, rest easy, and wake refreshed for another day's fearless travels.

Storing luggage

At times, you may want to leave your baggage behind and pick it up later. You can often do this at your hotel, a station, or airport. If you're passing through a big city or major crossroads where you intend to return, you can leave it there. For example, if you're heading first to the tropics and then to the mountains, why not leave cold-weather kit behind to pick up later? Or if you go on a shopping spree in the capital but don't want to carry your purchases around, leave them in the city and pick them up before your final flight. Make sure your bags are tagged with your name and details.

Keep a hotel business card

When you've been ambling around a foreign city all day, finding your way back to the hotel or directing a taxi to it can be a challenging proposition. To save yourself from having to sleep on the sidewalk, carry the hotel's business card to show to cab drivers, or to call the hotel for directions. Alternatively, the desk clerk will be used to travelers asking for a street map, and will be happy to mark the location of the hotel on it.

Should things go wrong

From time to time, hotels are bound to make mistakes, and you should complain. If a quality hotel is overbooked, they should arrange accommodation for you at another hotel and then either give you an upgrade or a discount to compensate. If you run into problems with the staff, take note of their names and ask to see their manager. Stay polite, but be firm. If a hotel room has a problem you can see, take photos. These let you bargain; public relations staff won't like the idea of your having such damning evidence of a problem in their hotel.

GIVE YOUR WALLET A BREAK

OK, it's true. Hotels generally have fixed rates, but there's often a surprisingly big gray area behind these supposedly "non-negotiation rules." A few bargaining tricks will frequently surprise you with great results.

Time it right: If you put some thought into your timing, you can score some amazing deals. This is especially true in areas dominated by peak tourist seasons, whether it's in the summertime, around festivals, or simply at school breaks. Prices are often higher at peak times. However, for the rest of the year, owners are more concerned with bringing in as many travelers as possible to fill the empty rooms. At these times, your business is valued enough so you can haggle over the price. For example, in tourist hotspot Cusco, in Peru, you can get a decent room for $5–$40 in February, but it can cost as much as $20–$100 in June when Cusco floods with sightseers en route to Machu Picchu.

Staying power: If you mean to hang your hat for a week or more somewhere, you can often get a discount, especially if the hotel is not filled.

Family matters: Hotel chains often have family discounts when you prearrange lodging. Ask about special deals, and inquire about how old children have to be to qualify.

Reward points: Frequent flyer miles and credit card points can often earn big discounts in hotel promotions. Check with your company by phone or visit its web site. You might be pleasantly surprised.

Honeymoon game: Playing the old honeymoon card is a well-worn trick to get some perks and treats from your lodging—be it a nicer room, a bottle of champagne, or the best table for dinner. But beware—this trick has been pulled by more than a few couples who were masquerading as honeymooners, so you may encounter some skepticism.

Stay in hostels: Hostelling International (HI) has thousands of locations in more than six dozen countries across the globe. They offer dorm beds and sometimes singles, doubles, and family rooms, too. If you take out membership with the association—you can sign up on arrival—it gives you a year's worth of low-rate accommodations and priority for reservations. They also throw in discounts to local attractions, too.

Pack a sense of humor

One golden rule is that you'll always get better service if you give the staff a smile, a warm thank-you, and the odd tip. It's cheap, easy, and you'll see instant results. Hotel owners and clerks are veritable mines of local knowledge and insider tips if you get on their good side.

4 Fearless
On the road

"For my part, I travel not to go anywhere, but to go. I travel for travel's sake. The great affair is to move"

ROBERT LOUIS STEVENSON

There's nothing quite like it: the wind's whipping through your hair, your blood's pumping, a knot of excitement is growing, and you exult in the feeling of leaving your humdrum, everyday life behind and having the whole world at your feet. Being on the road is what travel is all about.

There's no time when you're likely to feel more alive, free, and exhilarated—drinking in new sights, sounds, and experiences, witnessing incredible places, and broadening your horizons in a way you could never imagine from the comfort of your living-room armchair. Any traveler can rhapsodize for hours about the sheer thrill of being on the move.

TRAVELING IN OTHER LANDS— CRUCIAL TIPS FOR THE UNWARY

If there's one thing that threatens a fearless traveler's safe passage through far-flung lands, it's simple ignorance. The more you travel, the more wise you become about the ways of the world, but it's not necessary to be a weather-beaten backpacker who's been on the road for decades to stay safe. By researching your destination, consulting well-researched guidebooks, and absorbing the fearless tips below, you're unlikely to see trouble or get embroiled in damage control. You'll feel more confident and secure and have a more relaxed, fancy-free, and fearless trip.

Being fearless on the road does not mean letting go entirely—that would be like driving blindfold. It's also about being prepared, and taking small precautions to avoid falling victim to travel disasters and minimize the impact of bad occurrences if they do happen. So read on for timely tips and suggestions to smooth your path and help you enjoy your fearless travels to the utmost.

Tip someone off

Even if you are traveling solo, there's no need to go it entirely alone. Leave a rough itinerary with a friend at home and let them know whenever you change those plans. If you're going off for a trek, taking a cruise, or simply chilling out on a beach that's far removed from the nearest cyber-cafe, let someone know when you should be back. If you intend to come back to the same hotel, let the owner know so they can raise the alarm if necessary. If you go trekking in any national park, leave word in the park offices and don't forget to tell them your intended route. Keeping in touch with loved ones at home will also help their peace of mind.

Dress to impress

You'll find that people warm to you more quickly if you adapt your clothing to fit in. Of course, this does not mean you have to wear saris in Delhi or freeze your delicate parts in a Scottish kilt in the Highlands. It's enough for you to respect the local sensibilities. In some places, you'll cause offense by dressing too casually or skimpily, while in others, it doesn't matter. Bikinis, bare legs, and shoulders are frowned upon in most Muslim countries, and in many parts of Asia, local people also feel more comfortable if you are well-covered.

But don't dress to impress too much

If you're planning on traveling to a poor country or on spending time in less developed regions, think about dressing down for a little extra security. Looking affluent is advertising that you have wealth, and someone might decide that they want you to share it with them. If you don't stand out as a foreigner, you will attract less attention and less hassle.

If you try to blend in, you'll also avoid being a magnet for unwanted attention. When I was traveling in India, I started to wear salvar kameez—the traditional women's dress of a long shirt and trousers. This is ideal for the climate, but I also found that people treated me with more respect when I wore Indian clothes because it is considered a respectful way to dress and shows that you are making an effort to relate to the culture.

Safety tips and foiling thieves

Basic safety rules are mostly common sense. If you're carrying a wallet, don't keep it in your back pocket or it will be an open invitation to pickpockets. If you have a safe in your room, put your valuables in it. If the room doesn't have a safe and you feel uncomfortable leaving them with the reception desk at your hotel, take them with you. The safest method of carrying your passport, travelers' checks, and other valuables is in a money belt underneath your clothes.

You may worry that thieves are wise to cunning ploys such as these, but the truth is that most thefts are by opportunists. People only know the money's there if you flash it around. So carry the cash you'll need for the day separately, and never fish around in a money belt on the street. Whenever you want to buy something small or give money to someone, it's safer to extract the money from a small supply than peel it off a wad.

Money management

It's one of our worst travel fears: what if all our money, travel documents, and identification were snatched when we were far from home? This happened to two of my friends when they were traveling in Barcelona. Both women had put their passports, cash, and credit cards in the same handbag and set off to do some shopping. But they fell victim to a trend common in Spanish and Italian cities—a motorcyclist rode past, grabbed the bag, and zipped off in a flash.

Lots of clever alternatives to the classic money belt are available, including a wallet that you wear around your neck and under your top, or one you can strap around your leg, hang under your arm, or from your bra. You can buy "travel bras" with hidden compartments. There's even a frilly satin and lace half-slip available with security pockets for your valuables. If you want another cash stash to fall back on, how about sewing an inside pocket into your pants?

This is an important lesson: bags are always the first target of thieves. Avoid carrying valuable items in a handbag or daypack, if possible. If you are unlucky enough to have it snatched or to be mugged, you're going to lose much more than you would if your belongings were cunningly hidden.

Another experienced travel friend of mine once had her day-bag snatched in a busy bus terminal in Bolivia. At first, she was upset and angry at losing her travel snacks, book, and sweater, but she soon perked up. Her revenge was already complete: the bag-snatcher had run off with property worth just about $8, and all her valuables were safe because she had put them in hidden money belts she was wearing.

It also makes common sense to be wary at ATMs. Watch that no one is looking over your shoulder, and stow your money in a safe spot before ambling off.

Keep an eye on trouble spots

If there are areas you should avoid in a city or town, a guide-book will usually warn you. But don't forget your common sense, too, and avoid narrow alleys and badly lit streets. Often, the least safe areas are around train or bus stations in major cities. Transportation hubs tend to be gathering points for unsavory characters. Be extra vigilant around these places; you may be more vulnerable there, too, because you are probably concentrating on catching a train or bus. The typical station is a hive of activity and distractions. Thieves are well aware of this— that's one reason they hang out there. So hang on to your bags and stay on the ball.

Major tourist attractions can attract pickpockets, so keep your stuff well hidden and don't put your trust in people too easily. In a bar or restaurant, keep your bag close to you and tied around the chair or table leg. If you're on a long bus or train journey, you may frustrate thieves by locking your bag, backpack, or case onto the luggage rack.

Driven to distraction

Be especially wary if someone distracts you in the street. It's common for thieves to work in a team. One party gets your attention while the other helps himself to your stuff. Jostling, spitting, spilling drinks, or tapping you on the shoulder are all techniques used by street robbers, so be especially on your guard if someone seems to be trying to make you drop it.

Here is a classic example. A crowd of young children in Italy once took my father off-guard when we were traveling together. They swarmed around him grinning, laughing, and chattering away, asking him to take their picture, while their friend swooped in from behind to grab his wallet and disappeared like a flash of lightning. It was the most charming tactic for thievery that I've ever witnessed.

Coping with theft

If you do have something stolen, don't panic. Try to stay calm. A theft doesn't have to be a disaster if you can take it step by step. First, report it to the police and get a written police report. You'll need this to make an insurance claim. If your passport was taken, first report this to the police and then contact your nearest embassy or consular representative. Your embassy can also be helpful in a worst-case scenario. They are there to help, and they have seen it all before.

Recognizing a smooth operator

Don't let your fear of being ripped off lead you to mistrust everyone, but be careful whom you fully trust. You'll soon be able to sort the smooth talkers from the genuinely friendly people. Operators of the smoother variety tend to hang around touristy areas and approach you with a well-practiced spiel.

For example, when my friend was once in Sri Lanka, she passed a man in the street who exclaimed, "Hello! How are you?" She didn't recognize the man, but he said, "Don't you remember me? From your hotel?" He was appealing to her politeness and embarrassment at not recognizing him and was so convincing that she followed him into the market, only to be spat out 20 minutes later, with some overpriced spices.

You should also beware of accepting gifts of food or drink from strangers, particularly on train or bus journeys. More than one traveler has woken up later to discover the loss of a few hours and a lot of luggage. Your guidebook will advise you on tourist scams specific to your destination—whether it's gem-smugglers, fake dollars, bogus "taxes," or something else. Be especially careful in matters of money. Remember if you're offered a deal that sounds too good to be true, it probably is!

Be an "old hand"

If you have just arrived in town and a shopkeeper or someone you've just met on the street asks how long you've been there, tell them a few days, at least. If you say you've just arrived, you may be marking yourself as easy prey—you won't know the prices of things yet, and you might well be setting yourself up as a prime target for misinformation.

Shaking off pests

Traveling in certain areas inevitably brings unwanted attention and sales pitches. The worst thing you can do in these situations is to show interest in their wares. Once you do, you'll never be able to shake them off and may end up getting so aggravated that you resort to rudeness—and nothing shatters your vacation frame of mind more quickly. But sometimes you can enter into a straightforward transaction. For example, if you're in a confusing bazaar and keep getting hassled by would-be guides, hiring someone as a guide will keep all the others off your back. Just don't let your new guide lead you into shops supposedly owned by their nearest and dearest, because you'll be paying their commission on top.

Prepare before you go out

It's wise to avoid looking, or being, lost. Always work out your route or get an idea of your bearings before striking out. Memorize it so you won't have to consult your guidebook or map when you're walking—that advertises your vulnerability.

But don't be paranoid, either. Local people can be very helpful in pointing you in the right direction. One evening I got lost trying to find my way back to my guesthouse in a small West African town. It was confusing because there were few street-lights and everything looked the same in the dark. A local boy offered to walk with me, but we were not able to communicate well because he did not speak much French and I couldn't speak the local language. After we walked for a few minutes, I began to feel nervous and asked him where we were going. "I was following you!" he said. He thought that I knew the way and just wanted a companion to walk me there. I described some landmarks near the guesthouse and he led me to it. A much better method of finding your way home would be to familiarize yourself with the street layout during the day time so you won't get lost after dark.

Fearless females

As already noted in Chapter 1 there's no reason why women shouldn't travel alone with confidence and in safety. But, as at home, it's still a good idea for women to be extra protective of their safety. Follow your instincts and don't take unnecessary risks. As well as being wary of the type of cabs you use (*see* p.100,) you must also take care when choosing guides. Get a personal recommendation or use a well-established company.

When you check out your hotel room, ensure that the door is firmly lockable. And try to avoid arriving in a new place late at night—spend that bit of extra cash so that you can arrive in daylight. When you're walking around the streets, looking confident and positive also helps to deter hasslers from targeting you.

Avoiding amorous advances

Wherever you go, one of the biggest challenges for the solo female traveler is learning how to sidestep the chat-up routines of the local peacocks—preferably without ruffling too many feathers. If you stay calm and treat these would-be Romeos with good-humored panache, you'll feel far better.

For example, one of the chat-up lines that solo female travelers hear many times is, "So where is your husband?" Well, why not play along? If you aren't married, inventing a husband and family, preferably ones who are about to turn up, can save a tremendous amount of aggravation, especially in those countries where foreign women are considered to have "looser morals" than locals. The old wearing-a-wedding-band trick is also well used and effective, as long as your love-struck admirers are looking at your left hand rather than other parts of your anatomy.

If you're on the receiving end of catcalls and whistles, the best response is to ignore the provocation and stare straight ahead. However, if your pursuer persists, it's great to have learned a few ardor-smothering sentences in the local language—try phrases such as, "I'm married", "Please stop bothering me", or "My boyfriend is on his way to meet me".

In some countries, you can also appeal to the protective instincts of the locals, especially the older women, if you feel harassed. Once, in a small mountain town in the Andes, I was disturbed in my hotel by a drunken and lecherous man intent on sharing my room. I quickly shut the door on him, but the whole exchange left me feeling very vulnerable, so I discussed it with the female hotel owner and—to my surprise and relief—she promptly ejected the offending man from her hotel.

Another effective way to avoid unwanted attentions is wearing sunglasses in the street. The glasses let you avoid catching people's eyes and prevent you from inadvertently giving them the wrong impression.

USING LOCAL TRANSPORTATION

The mere act of traveling can be boring at times, but not if you set out to make it an adventure. Don't be scared of using the local travel systems—try a little of everything, it can really spice up the humdrum of getting from A to B!

Mix and match transport methods

It's much more fun to be flexible when you're travelling in a strange country. On one of my first long-haul trips in Southeast Asia, my companion and I became so bewitched by the new and exciting methods of getting around that we started keeping score of just how many types of local transportation we'd used. In fact, we began to go out of our way simply to experience brand new ways of travelling. We rode on three-wheeled, open-sided little tuk-tuks, rickshaws, motorboats, trucks, trains, longboats, motorbikes, 4-wheel drives, buses, canoes, horse-and-carts, taxis, ferries, bikes, and pretty much anything else that came along. And we had a fantastic time!

Even if you're highly familiar with a particular type of transportation at home, it will be a completely whole new experience abroad. Taking a whirl on different vehicles gives you a different point of view and provides different vantage points from which to see the world around you. Whether you're feeling like royalty—and not a little guilty—on the back of a hand-drawn rickshaw or clinging for dear life to a cantering camel, always try and make the most of whatever transportation choices are available.

Treat it as a cultural experience

Getting around on public transportation in a foreign country offers a far richer cultural experience than you would ever expect. This is one of times when you'll rub shoulders most closely with the local people and it's a shame to waste this golden opportunity. So step out of air-conditioned comfort and step on the local bus whenever you feel up to it.

When traveling in Latin America, I never took a bus, combi van, taxi, train, or boat without making some new friends or collecting amusing stories to scribble in my journal each night. The person I sat beside always struck up a conversation. Vendors would hop on and off at each stop and deliver a passionate spiel about the products—everything from "miracle cures" to candies— and their own poverty, trying to appeal to the hearts and minds of every passenger. There was always a subtle game of "seating politics" in overcrowded buses and trucks.

The elderly would claim seats from the young, and larger ladies would shuffle their bottoms across to nudge smaller travelers off their seat. There would be local music or horror films playing, children squabbling, and adults discussing politics. And the bus itself would often resemble a Christmas parade, with colorful decorations, flashing lights, fake flowers, and a Virgin Mary dangling in the windshield. On one occasion, the bus was even delayed by an hour because the driver was collecting his dinner from roadside vegetables that had fallen off the back of a truck.

What is everyday and mundane to the people who live in a place can be amazing to a stranger. When I was in India, I got into a women-only carriage at the front of a train—this is wonderful if you're a woman traveling alone. After some tenacious battling over seats, we settled down and crammed onto four bunks. As the journey started, the women began to chant religious songs while at the same time, fielding and bargaining with hawkers who were selling underwear, doilies, towels, and other items specially pitched at this female audience. To me, it was as bewitching an experience as visiting any temple.

Haggling for your ride home

For many forms of transportation, you will have to brush up your bargaining skills. Bargaining in lots of countries is the accepted means of agreeing on transactions. Some visitors find it difficult to argue over prices because they feel embarrassed. Try to overcome this—you'll not only pay less, but also keep inflation down for other tourists. Some tourists embrace it entirely too much and haggle till it hurts—remember that people are just trying to make a living and it's a social dance, not a steely contest of wills. If somebody is charging a ridiculous price or refusing to use their taximeter, if they have one, walk away. There are usually plenty more drivers who are only too happy to get your business. For more on all things mercenary, *see* "Shop 'Til You Drop" p.121.

Transportation with its own agenda

Competition for the tourist buck is always hot, but in some countries, it's ridiculous. On many occasions in India, Thailand, and North Africa, I asked the driver of a tuk-tuk (a motorized three-wheeled vehicle) to take me back to my hotel, to which he would reply, "Very good. But first, we see some shops, OK?" "Oh, no—just to my hotel please," I would respond. "All right, pay me a bit more and we'll just go to two shops," he came back with. "No thank you, just the hotel," I would insist patiently, at which point he would refuse point-blank to take me anywhere! The reason? Well, he was on commission.

The tourist stores are so keen to bring in the bucks that they pay drivers hefty commissions just for bringing the tourists to them. The drivers get so dependent on this extra income that they don't bother with the standard, less lucrative fares if they can help it! Don't worry though, there are always plenty more taxis in the city.

Taxi safety tips

When you're taking foreign taxis, check that the cab is registered and that the driver has a license. Your guidebook should fill you in on local taxi lore. For example, there are lots of unregistered taxis in London that lone travelers should avoid. Look for the official black cabs or go to a minicab office.

In some countries, there is a system of shared taxis. They take several customers at a time, each to a different destination. It's wise to be wary about getting into these cabs after dark, particularly if you are a woman. Women travelers should also sit in the back seat rather than the front. In Egypt, I sat in the front seat next to a kindly looking elderly taxi driver and was shocked when he leant across me ostensibly to do something to the door but actually to stroke my leg!

Also, don't be shy to ask to get out if you feel uncomfortable about the way your driver is behaving. But try to do this early so you aren't' stranded outside the town. For example, during a research trip in Venezuela, I hired a four-wheel drive taxi to take me to a distant mountain town. We had to travel along a winding, cliff-hanging road that fell steeply to the coast. I was somewhat unnerved when my driver stopped to buy a six-pack of beer and offered me one on our way out of town, but I reasoned that he was buying them for a later time. However, as it turned out, it's common for local drivers to drink a cold beer when they're driving. My driver went through no less than four just on our way up the mountain–and it was too late to ask to be let out. Imagine how I flinched each time we screeched around a corner on the narrow, cliff-hugging road!

Get a group together

It's easy to underestimate the paying power of traveling in a group. Even when traveling long distances, you'll be surprised how economically you can travel if you take taxis and invite some new travel buddies along for the ride. You can sometimes even save more money than you would have by going on the local bus or train. Imagine the luxury of not having to wait around for buses and trains to depart and being able to just hop into a cab that will drive you all the way to the next city—without having to dig too deeply into your wallet.

Communicating your destination

When I first visited Thailand, I was thrilled to scoot around Bangkok in the noisy little open-sided tuk-tuks that throng the streets. But we soon discovered that getting around when you don't speak the language could be a tough proposition. On several occasions we named the site we wanted to go to, the driver eagerly nodded, pleased to get the business, and we happily zoomed off to the opposite side of the city to our intended destination. We usually discovered the mistake too late and were stranded.

To avoid this sort of mix-up, ask the hotel staff to write down addresses and sites in the local lingo so there's no confusion. You could also show drivers a map or hotel business card, although drivers in some poor countries are illiterate. Don't despair! They can always ask passing people to translate for them. But don't automatically assume that the driver knows where he's supposed to be heading!

Get your own wheels

A fantastic way to explore new places is to rent a scooter or bike. This is much less expensive than renting a car and scooting around like a true adventurer can give you a tremendous buzz and feeling of independence. If you're in a city, try to do this on a Sunday when there's less traffic. Don't forget to rent a safety helmet, too.

Local lowdown

If you want to seek out where it's really at, you probably want to avoid entertainment at your hotel or resort, or shows or "authentic experiences" that are offered in touristy areas. That's not to dismiss these performances completely, but simply to point out that they are created and shown for tourists. If you want to get more of a local flavor, you'll have to head elsewhere. A savvy guidebook will help point you in the right direction, but there are lots of other ways of finding out too. Look out for local flyers and posters that advertize upcoming concerts. Local listings in magazines and newspapers are mines of information.

Asking around is another way of keeping your ear to the ground. But bear in mind that people working at your hotel, guides, or taxi drivers may be working on commission, so you might need to treat recommendations with caution. Talking to other travelers is a great way to find out where it's hot and where it's not because they may have experienced something fantastic and will always be eager to share this knowledge.

SIGHTSEEING TIPS

If something is feted as a national treasure, there's a good reason behind all the fanfare. Don't fall into the trap of not bothering to go and see something because you assume it can't possibly live up to the clamor of all the hype. For example, the Taj Mahal in India will certainly exceed your expectations, even though it adorns a million teatowels, lit-up plastic models of it are on every tourist-shop counter, and a hungry tourist town surrounds it. The Pyramids remain incredible even though their fame makes them eerily familiar and there's a hubbub of coach tours and hopeful camel drivers surrounding them.

Contemporary Cairo snaps at the heels of the Sphinx—this is the fate of many such sights. But frequently you'll find that their splendor is compounded, rather than undermined, by the ordinariness of the hustling, bustling cities that have grown toward and around them.

Avoiding the crowds

Even when you visit the most popular attractions, you can often give the crowds the slip. These sights frequently open very early in the morning; if you're the first to get there, you may miss the rush hour. I visited the Taj Mahal twice: once in the late afternoon and evening to watch the sun set and again to see the sun rise the next morning. In contrast to the confusing mayhem of mid-afternoon, at sunrise the complex was completely deserted and was utterly captivating in the pale, fluid hues of the early morning.

This tactic also worked when I visited Blarney Castle in Cork, Ireland—the resting place of the famous Blarney stone that inspires those that kiss it with the "gift of the gab". In summer, tourists swarm this castle and it can take an hour or more in line before you can kiss the legendary stone at the top of the castle. But by arriving first thing in the morning, before the sun had fully risen, my friend and I were treated to seeing the castle at its best. The grounds were still shrouded in morning mist, glistening with dew, and best of all, totally deserted except for us and the birds.

Always remember that the local lunch hour is a good visiting time. Whether you're skiing on the Alps, trooping around the Tower of London, or heading to the Colosseum in Rome, fewer people will be around. Toward the end of the day is another good bet.

Avoid visiting places on days when they will be packed full of other tourists. And watch out for public holidays, festivals, or religious days. By all means avoid Nôtre Dame in Paris, France, during the Easter break, unless lines do it for you. Also watch for special prices or times with free admission. If a museum has a free-of-charge day every week, that's when they will be most crowded—decide whether the price cut is worth the lines you'll probably encounter.

Keep an eye on the clock

Once when I visited the Pyramids, I got there—through bad planning—late in the afternoon when they were just about to close. My friend and I rented two horses from an Egyptian who told us we could ride into the Pyramid enclosure, although it turned out that this was not permitted. He came with us and when we spotted police patrolling the area on their camels, he commanded us to gallop away—it was easy for the horses to outpace the camels. Although this was an unconventional way to visit the Pyramids, it was a glorious way to see them. The crowds had dispersed and the sun was setting. And there was an extra frisson of excitement in having to gallop away from the camels on patrol.

In this instance, I was lucky not have a wasted journey, but it's wiser to check the opening and closing hours of attractions. If you don't have long in a particular place, it's terribly frustrating to arrive somewhere just as it closes. Check to see if there are times when an attraction is open late. For example, many museums are open into the evening hours on certain days, and this is a prime time to visit because they are rarely crowded then. At the same time, check to see when a site is closed. To make things easier, countries tend to have a single day when all museums are shut—usually Sunday, Monday, or Tuesday. If you visit a town with nothing else in it but a famous temple and discover that the temple is closed that day, you'll feel like kicking yourself.

Hidden secrets

Seeking out lesser-known attractions may take more effort, but is well worth it. Taking a leap off the beaten track will immediately land you in a less crowded, less sullied, more intriguing domain. A guidebook may be able to point you away from the main tourist haunts, but other travelers can be tremendous mines of information on even less-discovered places. When I was in India, a traveler told me about a guest-house that offered a three-day trekking trip to some remote villages. He had returned that day. The trip didn't appear in the current guidebooks,so not many travelers had visited the area. These kind of gems, up-to-date and first hand, are fantastic.

Local people may tell you about places worth visiting. Again, be wary if they also happen to be working in the tourist trade. However, your inborn garbage detector usually kicks into motion and helps sort the value of particular pieces of advice. In a small town in Wales, a pottery shop owner told me about a fantastic ruin half-a-mile from the town. His enthusiasm was so great that I had to go to find it—following the map that he had drawn for me on a scrap of paper. He was right. It was an extraordinarily beautiful ruined house nestled in a valley—with trees growing up through it.

The local press and listings magazines also tell you about seemingly secret places. You can find out about temporary exhibitions or one-time-only events that you might otherwise miss. Ask at your hotel or check a guidebook to find out about useful local publications. For example, in Paris, France, the weekly *Pariscope* lists information about what's currently showing, *Time Out* does the same job in London, England, while the *Cairo Times* in Cairo, Egypt, is an English-language weekly that lists local live music happenings.

Take a leap into the unknown

Guidebooks are excellent companions for discovering a new country, but once you've found your feet, don't ever feel that you have to stick to them. In some countries, the mere mention of a town in a popular guidebook will turn it into a hive of tourist activity. It can therefore be more enlightening to take a walk on the "wild side" and make a point of visiting places not listed in a guidebook. But this doesn't have to mean a major expedition. Even escaping into the countryside to a tiny village for an hour or two can yield fantastic insights into the rhythm of the country's traditional life.

Once, when traveling in Ecuador, I met a quirky Australian man who proudly claimed to navigate purely by chance. He'd visit the bus station, look at the names on the front of the buses and pick the one he liked the sound of most! You may say he was a crazy hobo—he'd be the first to admit it—but he certainly saw a different side to the countries he visited.

Experience a different life

On the same note, you don't learn about a place only through dusty museums, staged shows, and guided tours. You can get surprising and memorable insights in even the most mundane of everyday situations. For example, going to the local movie theater after a hard day sightseeing not only gives your feet a welcome break, but is a cultural experience in itself. Note the way the theater is organized, the film is presented, and especially how the audiences react. Likewise, turning on your hotel TV and watching local TV channels yields some funny moments such as the dramatic drum rolls, big hair, and close-ups of a Latin American *telenovela* (soap opera) or the traditional finery that local music groups wear when they perform. How about getting your hair cut in a different country? When in Colombia, my cousin went to get a haircut with a part-time bullfighter who was happily chatting away about killing bulls while wielding sharp scissors above her head.

> *You'll be surprised how many of the most memorable moments from traveling come from simply stepping out of your tourist shoes and stepping into those of the local people for a while.*

Take it in your stride

While it's possible to plan and plan, remember that you can never guarantee a hundred percent smooth passage when traveling. An element of unpredictability is part and parcel of the adventure. You can never know when a theater, museum, or temple is closed for repairs, when there will be a transportation strike, an area flooded by torrential rain, a snowfall that prevents passage, or any number of other crises. As John Steinbeck put it, "A journey is like marriage. The certain way to be wrong is to think you control it."

5 *Fearless*
Shopping, eating & hanging out

"...I have learned that the cost of everything from a royal suite to a bottle of soda water can be halved by the simple expedient of saying it must be halved."

ROBERT BYRON

Once you're settling into the traveling routine like the fearless traveler you are, it's time to have some real fun! Shopping for souvenirs, partaking of the local delicacies, plus getting to know the local people and other travelers are some of the most exciting and memorable experiences you'll have. Read on for tips on making the most of the opportunities that come your way.

You'll collect far more rewarding experiences if you immerse yourself in the local culture. Break away from the tour group and talk with the locals, take the local transportation, taste the local specialties, and shop in the outdoor markets and the local grocery stores. Befriend the hotel staff to learn the gossip about what the locals do for kicks. Once you've started on your journey of discovery there will be no stopping you.

Fearless foodies

Trying foreign foods can be daunting. Some travelers avoid the local gastronomy as something suspicious. But for fearless travelers, it's a great opportunity—one not to be missed. This is your chance to partake in new and exotic flavors, textures and aromas; to taste something you've never tasted before on almost every day of your trip. Even if you think you've eaten your fill of foreign food in your own country, remember that dining in your local curry house will not prepare you for the real thing, packed with the freshest local produce and spices, and ingrained with centuries of tradition.

Enjoying the local cuisine is not just an exercise in taste-bud tickling: food and eating are inescapably intertwined with the local culture. You'll learn what foods signify in each culture, how they are eaten, plus the rituals and customs surrounding meals. Did you know that in many cultures, rice is a symbol of purity and fertility? Or that Andean maize is still "sacrificed" to honor the gods? In Turkey, people are so passionate about food they write odes to yogurt and pop songs about fish sandwiches.

There's so much to discover about foods around the world that you could write a vast library on the subject. So go on, be a fearless foodie and dig in!

Cooking up a treat

If you're a cook or just enjoy learning new skills, taking a cooking class in another country can be a wonderfully rewarding experience. And when you go home, you can make the most authentic curry or garlic snails in your neighborhood and also have a tasty way to recall your trip.

What to choose

When you're confronted with a menu filled with a long list of unfamiliar and exotic sounding dishes, it can be difficult to make a decision that's not pure potluck. If you can speak the language, question the waiter to find out which are the specialties and typical dishes of the region. Guidebooks usually have a useful glossary and menu decoder, too. Alternatively, look at what everyone else is eating. If something appeals to you, point at it. Don't be embarrassed—the waiter will know exactly what you're saying.

Communication

When the phrasebook or "pointing-and-nodding" methods fail and you have something specific in mind, try taking along a traveler's picture dictionary. It sounds odd, and it looks odd—something like a children's picture book with clear photos of every basic foodstuff and other necessities of travel, from chicken to eggplant to stamps. It might make you cringe, but it works. No more asking for ice cream and getting eggnog soup instead!

Far from the madding crowd

If you're visiting a place with many tourists, look beyond the center to find authentic, cheaper meals where you'll be rubbing shoulders with the locals. Don't be timid about going into those dingy little side-street cafes that seem to have a conspiratorial air, or the street stalls that sell freshly sizzled concoctions to the locals. But do use common sense and read your guide-book for advice about the street foods that are safe for the adventurous traveler—and get them while they're hot.

Saving cents

If you're concerned about the hole that's appearing in your wallet from eating out during trips abroad, try a few of these money-saving tricks.

Have a picnic: Why not dive into the nearest bakery or delicatessen and put together a tasty picnic to munch on while you're sitting on a park bench, an old stone wall, or even on the beach? It'll save you from shelling out on restaurants, and as a bonus you can watch local life unfold around you.

Penny-pinching portions: Some countries habitually serve enormous portions of food. My cousin Emma and I stayed with local families in Ecuador, and Emma discovered that Ecuadorian meals are so big that the 6-year old daughter of the house ate twice as much as she did! In most Latin American countries, you can buy very cheap—but enormous—set meals with three courses. Emma and I shared each set meal, and it was more than sufficient for both of us. That way, we often paid the grand sum of about 50 cents each. If you're not sure how big the portions will be in your destination, try finding a local restaurant and look around at what the other diners are eating before making your choice.

Eat at the counter: In some restaurants and cafes, you'll be given the choice of eating at a table or grabbing a quick meal or snack sitting or standing at the bar. This is especially true in Europe, particularly in France and Spain. In these situations, opt for the bar because it's usually less expensive.

Make the most of the cuisine

Even if you're traveling on a tight budget or are on a diet, remember that you may never come back to this country, so make the most of local delicacies while you can. Food is integral to your enjoyment and understanding of the locality, so treat yourself. Splurge on some really great restaurants and deliciously sinful food. It doesn't have to be a daily occurrence, but you'll be missing something special if you don't treat yourself occasionally. You're on vacation after all. Remember that you may never get the opportunity to taste fresh Argentinean steak or Italian ice cream again. Go on—spoil yourself!

Daring eats

Indulging in local specialties is one thing, but some are more of a challenge than others. Visitors to the Amazon are usually shocked when they are offered deep-fried, fat-bottomed ants to chew on. Similarly, spicy jellyfish in Korea, Venezuelan lizard broth, or Australian crocodile meat may not be what you had envisioned for dinner. But if you can stomach such local peculiarities, it's a great adventure—and it does make a great story to tell your friends at home.

Getting invited

One of the most rewarding and insightful experiences a traveler can have is to befriend a local and be invited to their home for a meal. You'll be surprised how often it happens. In many cultures, food is the principal means of showing hospitality to strangers and guests—and it's a tasty way to make friends. You'll also see another side to the local cuisine because what people cook in their homes is often different than what you will find in restaurants.

Whining and dining

Taking kids out in foreign restaurants can be a mammoth test of your patience. Your little cherubs may be very suspicious of foreign food and may refuse to eat it at all. To ease this concern, introduce the country's cuisine while you're still at home. Today, it's usually possible to find some form of most world cuisines at the local supermarket, an ethnic market, or as takeout from a restaurant. And as a backup when you're traveling, it's wise to bring along some of their favorite foods. When the fidgets are really bad, try ordering take out or room service—you might even be able to find a restaurant with an attached playground!

Of course, it's especially important to pick up on local etiquette when eating at a friend's home. Wherever you go, there are social rules of decorum associated with eating——whether it is keeping your mouth closed while you are chewing or never using the left hand to eat, as in India. In some Asian regions, it's even a compliment to the chef to give a satisfied burp after the meal!

Check the check

Mistakes happen all around the world, but in some countries it's almost accepted that the meal check will be "boosted" in some fashion. Don't ever lose your temper in these circumstances. Treat it like a game and respond by pointing out the error with good-humored panache. Your waiter will generally smile, wink, and correct the bill without a peep.

Tipping

Travelers often wonder, "How much should I tip the waiter?" This is different in every culture. To avoid looking stingy or losing all your cash to tips, check the advice in your guide-book or watch how much local diners leave on their tables.

Don't expect familiar food

In addition to enhancing your travel experience, eating the local food also helps to avoid being disappointed. Restaurants may add American or European favorites to their menu to tempt tourist dollars. But remember that it's not their specialty. I once visited such a restaurant with a menu written in English. It advertised simple dishes such as "fried egg." I ordered one and settled down to wait for my breakfast. When it finally came, it turned out to be a hard-boiled egg that had then been shelled and fried in oil, still in one greasy piece.

 Healthy eating tips

Try not to feel overly paranoid about food-hygiene standards, because exploring the local cuisine is a central part of any travel experience. That said, it's sensible to take a few simple precautions to avoid problems. Even when hygiene standards are good, your stomach may take a while to adjust to the new foods, especially if they have a lot of spices. In these circumstances, try to ease yourself into the local diet slowly, starting off with relatively bland food.

Always insist on freshly cooked food, especially from street stalls. Vegetables and fruit should be washed in pure water and peeled before eating. Be wary of shellfish and other seafood. Check that tap water is safe to drink—before drinking it. If it's not, order drinks without ice cubes (usually made with tap water.) Also beware ice cream sold on the street —it may have been refrozen.

Tips for the vegetarian

Vegetarians often have problems communicating that they don't eat meat. Never assume that people understand the concept of vegetarianism. Meat is such a central part of the diet in many cultures that the idea of choosing not to eat it is totally alien. You may take it for granted that "no meat" rules out fish, chicken, and soup stock made with animal fats, but not everyone will make this distinction. Many a time friends have requested a vegetarian dish, only for it to arrive with bits of ham sprinkled over the top or, on one occasion, a whole chicken foot floating in a bowl of noodle soup.

To avoid any nasty surprises, be specific. Rather than asking, "Is this dish vegetarian?" say, "Does this have any meat, chicken, fish, or animal fat?" Don't forget to ask the same thing about every dish—even that leafy salad may come with a meaty garnish. If the waiter appears unsure, ask the cook directly.

Eating solo

Traveling on your own is a wonderfully liberating experience, but there are always moments when you feel your solitude more sharply than others. On my long research trips, I find that the time when I miss my travel buddies most is when I'm eating out in restaurants. Dinner is often the perfect time to relive the excitement of your day, relaxing and laughing over a post-dinner drink. Sitting alone makes you hypersensitive to all the happily squabbling families and laughing friends at the tables around you. Of course, it's a great chance to observe people, but you may also feel a little out of place.

Taking along a book or newspaper always lessens this feeling, as does chatting to staff when they're not busy. Alternatively, you could take the opportunity to mingle with the locals, maybe ordering bar food and chewing the fat with the barman and other bar flies. Don't be shy—this will make you feel like a truly fearless traveler.

Discover the local food market

There's nothing so vibrant and colorful as the local food marketplace, bazaar, or souk. These are the community's most active sites of social interaction, where you'll find one and all bargaining over the country's most typical foodstuffs. You could spend hours simply wandering around and watching the vendors in action. But as well as providing a peephole into the heart of the local culture, markets charge a fraction of the prices in stores, supermarkets, and restaurants. It's a win-win situation for travelers. Wandering around at the local market is also a great way to get your culinary bearings in a new culture. Explore the piles of diverse vegetables, browse the sacks of staples, and smell the varied aromas. Try a little of all the exotic fruits before you buy them—stallholders will love introducing you to each. You'll often be amazed by the sheer variety, from the 500 types of Indian mangos to the close to 4000 varieties of Peruvian potatoes. You'll find them all in the market.

SHOP 'TIL YOU DROP

A fun highlight of traveling is picking out keepsakes. Wherever your travels take you, you're bound to see all sorts of fabulous souvenirs that make your wallet hand twitch. But how can you tell which pieces are authentic? And how do you know that you're being charged the right price? Just follow some top tips for the fearless traveler.

Take your time

When you first arrive in a new country, everything sold in the markets and souvenir shops looks new, exotic, and tempting. However, it pays to hold back from buying until you've got your bearings. Today, many of the handicrafts are made just for tourists, and quality, authentic craft goods are harder to find. The paintings sold on "papyrus" paper in Egypt are more often daubed on banana leaves than the genuine article. Wooden statuettes may be covered with shoe-polish to make the wood look old. Those baby alpaca slippers from the Andes may be bleached rabbit fur.

The more time you spend exploring and asking questions, the better you'll be able to recognize the authentic crafts. Spend time browsing, looking at different handicrafts, and learning about their quality and prices. Ask other travelers what they've bought, from where, and how much it cost. Befriend locals and ask them what they would buy and how much they would expect to pay. Then, when you're finally ready to become a buyer, you're assured of getting a good deal.

What to buy?

When you're thinking about which souvenirs to buy, spare a thought to what packs easily. Local clothing and jewelry are especially good souvenirs that you won't find anywhere else, and they won't take up too much space in your bags. If you really cannot resist that Australian didgeridoo or Kashmiri carpet, put off buying it until the end of your trip if possible, or be prepared to fork out for the cost of mailing it home. Going shopping with a friend also introduces the voice of reason—good friends will be able to talk you out of unwise purchases.

The best souvenirs

Remember that you needn't spend a fortune in fancy souvenir shops to take home treasured keepsakes. My favorite souvenirs are often the simpler items. For example, I'll never forget traveling through soccer-crazy South America during the World Cup and I treasure my canary yellow Ecuador football shirt for the memories associated with it.

Some travelers make a hobby out of collecting everyday things like unusual cigarette packets or matchboxes. Pick up whatever appeals to you. I sometimes collect low-denomination currency, beer labels, and kitsch postcards, which I paste into my journal. But anything that jogs your memory is a great keepsake.

The best free souvenir I ever took home was one that the customs men may have raised an eyebrow over had they found it. On the banks of an alligator-infested Bolivian river, I found a complete alligator skull and decided, almost certainly against my better judgment, that it would look wonderful on my mantelpiece. It certainly does look striking, although it scared my poor granny almost to death!

Keep on top of the currency

It's easy to lose track of how much you're spending in a foreign country. We've all been seduced by the siren call of souvenir shops. It's equally easy to be shortchanged by cabbies accustomed to disorientated tourists who haven't gotten down to grips with the exchange rate. I usually print a pocket-card sized conversion chart—available on websites such as www.oanda.com—which I keep in my wallet. It's far less awkward than juggling a calculator and is a timely reminder when I open my wallet to pay for items I can't honestly afford.

Buy personally made items

Such is the modern global market that it's not uncommon to find African-style souvenir statuettes that have been mass-produced in India or "Egyptian" vases that were actually made in Taiwan. The souvenir trade is so lucrative in some tourist areas that you can't tell which are the authentic, locally-produced pieces or which ones will profit the craftsmen and not just line the pockets of the big-shot merchants.

For these reasons, it's always best to buy direct from the craftsman or at least from the region in which the craft is produced. You can be assured of authenticity and also that you are paying local people who need your money more than do the owners of big tourist-trap shops in the cities. You'll also feel a much closer connection with the items you're buying, having seen where they come from and how they are made. Besides, the crafts will be a fraction of the price. So buying directly from the producer makes you a winner all around.

Fearless bargaining

In many developing countries, bartering is the accepted way of doing business. You'll be able to haggle for everything from taxi fares to exquisite handicrafts at the market or even antiques in an upper-crust store. Haggling is a useful skill, not to mention a great deal of fun to practice.

The more you do it, the more comfortable and easy it becomes. Don't worry if you suffer the occasional bad deal. These guys are professionals and their living depends on their bartering ability. For them it's a battle of wits and determination, and they have a hundred arguments and bargaining ploys. Just remember that most of what you hear is clever salesmanship and don't take any of it too seriously. The important thing is to have fun—and hopefully not lose too much money in the process!

Bargaining can also be a memorable cultural interchange. In many cultures it's an opportunity to sit down with a cup of tea, some wine, or to smoke a pipe. It's a chance to chew the fat and, for the vendor, an opportunity to soften you up and encourage you to relax. In Egypt, you'll be invited back to merchants' homes to sample the local hospitality, and in India, you'll be asked to sit down for a cup of sweet, milky tea and asked about your family and how you like the country. Vendors are happy to help you out and offer advice in the hope that you'll then favor them with your business, so enjoy it. Milk the opportunity and their insider tips.

Check local norms

Of course, the rules and ethics of haggling change from country to country, so keep your ears and eyes open to see how the locals handle themselves when haggling. Most guidebooks suggest some rules for bargaining, too, but don't expect everyone's tactics to match.

It varies from a little friendly horse-trading to merciless, brow-beating bartering. Check in your guidebook or ask locals what you can and can't bargain for in each country. Can you haggle in fancy stores as well as in the local market? Once you have got the basic idea, you can get out there and brush up your bartering skills.

 The price is right

The best way to avoid falling foul of a bad bargain is to do your homework. If you know the going rate for the object of your desire, you'll go into a bartering session fearless and forearmed. You'll also want to establish an idea of quality—because many of the more dishonest vendors rely on the ignorance of tourists. If you can demonstrate your knowledge, you'll win a whole new respect from your haggling partner.

Don't rush in and buy the first desirable item you see. Note prices in a few shops and check out the market to see what other people are paying. Ask other travelers what they have bought, where they shopped, and how much they paid. If you can resist for long enough, put off your shopping sprees until the end of the trip, when you'll have collected enough information on prices and quality to grapple with even the hardest of hagglers.

If you don't know the going rate, some people recommend that you offer half what the vendor says, although this isn't a hard-and-fast rule. I've known vendors to ask for five times the value and more. One cheeky Egyptian even asked $45 for a vase worth just $4 in the local market. Of course, the default bargaining strategy is simply to bargain and bargain until the vendor will go no any lower, even after you have walked away. But this can be a lengthy process. So it's best to do your research, haggle hard, know your desired price range, and to do it all with a smile on your face.

Be willing to walk away

It's a fact—market vendors are able to sniff out an interested customer a mile off. And if you show overt signs of interest in any product, you may find yourself at their mercy. Haggling is often a subtle acting game, so play along. If you see something you like, feign indifference. Ask the prices of several different items, only one of which interests you. Say a polite thank-you and good-bye, then shuffle away slowly and check prices for similar items on nearby stalls.

Any vendor worth their salt will save their best price for the moment when you actually leave. I've had salesmen run after me crying a lower price for every yard I walk away. In fact, I once struck my best-ever bargain this way—a beautiful footstool from the Amazon. I walked away, telling the enthusiastic vendor that I didn't want it, but he kept following me, bringing the price down and down. In the end, he made me an offer I just couldn't refuse.

Don't be bullied

The hard-nosed hagglers of some countries don't so much barter as bully their customers into buying goods. It sounds dramatic, but you may feel honor-bound to buy goods simply because of the sheer energy and commitment someone has put into selling it to you.

On one of my first trips around Asia, my friend and I were drawn into a Kashmiri carpet store out of curiosity and with no intention of buying anything. But we weren't prepared for the tornado-like sales pitch that we received the second we stepped in the door. We were pounced upon, manhandled on to a seat, given tea we hadn't asked for, and forced to listen to an impassioned speech about how wonderful our home country was, and what a special deal he would be prepared to give us on his carpets because he liked us so much!

Insulting the merchandise

Never insult the vendor, but do try criticizing the wares to lower the asking price. This is standard practice in the Middle East. As soon as you make a comment about a particular shawl— that it's not fit to line the dog's bed, for example—the vendor will take the cue to launch into a well-rehearsed speech about what good value it is. So take your cue, inspect the item closely, frown, purse your lips, smile wryly at the vendor's sales pitch, and run your fingers thoughtfully over any blemish. Bartering is a game or social dance, and this is not considered rude. So relax, enjoy yourself, and play along.

Dressing down

Dress like an affluent tourist, and you're at an immediate disadvantage with savvy vendors. If you've hooked a designer handbag on your arm, flashy sunglasses on your head, and a clutch of freshly purchased goods under your arm, sales-people will instantly pick you as a high-spender and charge accordingly. So dress down when you head for the market.

Control your cash

How you treat hard cash when bargaining can be an effective weapon or a huge hindrance. It helps to store money in separate places so that you don't flash heaps of cash before a deal is made—that always jacks up the asking price. If you already have a particular price in mind, lay it out for the vendor to see. Sellers sometimes can't resist the sight of cold, hard cash and you'll often get a fairer deal more quickly this way.

Cutting a deal

It's an advantage if you can find several of the things you want in one shop. A potentially big sale can delight a shopkeeper so much that the overall price gets lower. If you'd like to buy a large quantity of something, start by haggling down the price of one item. Then ask if the price will go lower for two, three, and so on. This is when you'll save some serious bucks and put more spending money back into your vacation pot.

A note about notes

Though carrying large-denomination notes may prevent your wallet from bulging, it can cause problems in some rural areas, especially in poorer countries. If you're buying fruit in a market, a note equivalent to $5 results in you or the proprietor running from stall to stall to find someone with change. If no one has any, you're out of luck. Banks usually give you high-denomination bills, so ask for smaller notes. Also check that none are old or torn, as they'll be rejected in many countries.

Mailing it home

If you're on a long trip, you won't want to be carrying that impulsively purchased haul of ceremonial masks all around Indonesia. So if you can't wait until the end of your trip to buy, consider mailing your purchases home. Some souvenir shops offer to mail your purchases home for a fee. Only do this if you are certain it's a reliable establishment. Shops have been known to substitute items of lower quality or mail them in a cheap and unreliable fashion, after charging you for airmail. Just remember that you'll need to keep your receipts and fill in the necessary forms at the airport.

Claiming tax back

Yes, that's right. In some countries you can claim cash back at customs for certain purchases as you leave the country. If you have spent a lot on vacation splurges, you may be pleasantly surprised to discover that you're not quite stone-broke. You get money back because as a foreign traveler, you are not liable for all of the taxes levied on the products. Of course, the rules vary from country to country, so check in your guidebook or with the tourist office. You could also ask the salesman if you're buying in a store that caters to tourists.

HANGING OUT

One of the most positive things about traveling is its potential to break down the barriers of suspicion and ignorance between cultures. You have the power to make friends, learn about alternative ways of living, and leave a good impression about your country. So be an ambassador. Respect the locals, their customs, and their rules of social decorum. Wear respectable clothes and always remain polite and interested in everything. Above all, remember that one person's wrong is another's right and show tolerance at all times.

This will not only ease your journey, but will also help to lessen any negative impacts of tourism. You can find out about local dos and don'ts by reading about the country and the culture—a guidebook usually spells out any taboos. Frequently these will be related to behavior. For example, in Muslim countries expressions of affection in public are deemed offensive. And the Venezuelans hold the South American Liberator Simón Bolívar in such regard that it is considered offensive to put your feet up on a bench or carry large objects in a plaza presided over by his statue. By all means talk about your country and the differences with other places, but never ever imply that your country is better, even if your hosts are criticizing their own country. You win far more friends by concentrating on the positive things about wherever you are.

Learn a little local lingo

It's extraordinary what a big difference it makes to learn a few words of the native language. Not only does it make getting around much easier and make you less likely to be taken for a ride, but people's attitudes towards you transform if you make a little effort with their language. It doesn't matter if you don't speak perfectly. Just trying shows a willingness to interact with the locals, to be more than just another tourist. Even basic words and phrases such as "hello", "goodbye", "please", and "thank you", along with "Do you speak English?" are enough to elicit a warm response to your questions.

I once found myself in a dead-end Thai town, miles from anywhere. I was in need of a bathroom but when I asked locals where I could find one, they seemed not to understand me. However, I dug out my phrasebook, memorized the question in Thai, and repeated it back to a girl I had asked earlier. I've never seen a face transform so quickly. It changed from stony disinterest to ecstatic joy as she exclaimed, "Ah, you speak Thai!" And then, in perfect English, she promptly told me where to find a bathroom.

Carry conversation kick-starts

A picture is worth a thousand words. So why not take along a few photos of your life at home: your family, friends, hobbies, pets, and your city or town. Pull them out and show them to your new friends when you run out of things you can say in their language. It gives them an easy glimpse into your culture. Often, they are amazed by details you take for granted.

Take something fun

You can also make friends in foreign climes more easily if you have something fun to offer. Some travelers take along small musical instruments like harmonicas or kazoos to break the ice with local kids and their families. Others take along a small tub of bubble soap and blow bubbles for the local kids. You'll be amazed how easily a little game can break down cultural barriers when there are children around. Showing your warmth for the children will soon allay any suspicions the adults feel.

One word of caution: in some countries, children have come to expect candies from travelers, so in some places you'll be followed by a chorusing group of children eager to get more such goodies. Please don't give in and compound this problem—aside from any other consideration, remember that poorer countries rarely have a surfeit of dentists.

Hang with the locals

We all have a mental list of sights and experiences we want to enjoy in a different country, but whatever your preferred itinerary, make a little time for something that locals—not just tourists—do. Immerse yourself in a local cultural event and soak up the atmosphere when the barriers of "us" and "them" are down. You could take yourself to a sports game, concert, movie, or dance performance. If you're religious, visiting a local church, mosque, or synagogue can be unforgettable.

Even the seemingly most familiar event, such as a baseball or soccer match, can be an entirely different experience abroad. For instance, baseball in a small town in Venezuela is a wonderful sight. Venezuela is baseball crazy, and a town just isn't a town without a diamond or full-blown stadium. But best of all is a children's variation of the game called *pelota de goma*. This literally means rubber ball, and uses the fist instead of the bat. It takes place anywhere, and pretty much everywhere, at the drop of a hat.

Similarly, going to a local soccer match in Latin America is amazing. When going to a match between two Bolivian league teams, I realized that football was as much a social occasion there as it was a sporting event. While the men shouted themselves hoarse and stomped their feet in support of their team, the boys ignored the match and kicked their own football around. Meanwhile, whole families were parking their bottoms on the concrete stands while they ate picnics, gossiped, and screamed with laughter.

Mixing with other travelers

Perhaps you're traveling with a tour group, staying in a hostel dorm room with other travelers, or traveling solo and want to meet other people with whom to travel. How should you approach them? Well, everyone has their own style, but why not take along a few games to break the ice? For example, you can buy soft, foldaway Frisbees in game and camping stores; they take virtually no room to pack and you can whip them out at any moment to start an impromptu game. Travelers can also be fanatical card players, so take a deck and learn a few simple card games before heading off.

Of course, if games aren't your scene, there's nothing that travelers enjoy better than swapping tales of their adventures. Start them off, and you probably won't be able to stop them!

Partying—do and don't

Do: You're on vacation to have a ball, so don't hold back when you're in a party mood. And if you enjoy a good boogie, never pass up an opportunity to go dancing. In some places, it's a crucial cultural experience, and even if, like me, you have two left feet, joining in to dance a Latin-American salsa or an Irish jig will be a bewitching experience you'll never forget.

Partying is also a wonderful way to mingle with the locals. Music, dancing, and a wee drop of the local tipple never fail as icebreakers. To make sure you're going to the hippest venues in the locality, ask the hotel staff where to find the best nightlife, or check the local press.

Another useful tip for party animals: If you're newly arrived in town, it's wise to bring a map in your pocket so you can find your way back after a few beers.

Don't: Drink and security don't mix. Most crimes against travelers happen after dark, and especially after a few drinks when their judgment is altered and their defenses are down. But you don't have to forgo your fun to be safe. Just take a few extra precautions. If you're going to have a big night out, take only what you need and leave your valuables somewhere safer than on your tipsy person. And don't go out drinking alone if you can possibly help it. Stick to well-lit areas, and keep a small cash stash somewhere for an emergency cab-ride back to the hotel. For obvious reasons, it's not smart to have a big night out before a long bus or plane journey.

Law abiding

It's important to remember that you're an ambassador for your country and a certain code of behavior is expected. The most obvious aspect of respecting a local culture is to be aware of its laws. More than a third of US citizens incarcerated abroad are held on drug charges. Some have been arrested for carrying prescription drugs that are illegal in other countries. On one occasion, my friend Rob found himself in hot water simply for carrying a friend's packet of powdered pancake mix across the Israeli-Egyptian border! So don't take any risks, and don't carry packages over borders.

Be fearless and friendly

Being overly paranoid about safety is one of the easiest and saddest mistakes a traveler can make. It will spoil your trip by making you worry needlessly and can prevent you from accepting the many kindnesses of strangers. After all, interacting with and befriending locals is often the best experience a traveler can have—don't rob yourself of it!

I first arrived in Latin America having read about the drug problems, kidnappings, armed robberies, and petty thefts. I don't doubt the depth of these problems, but in all my many travels there, I've rarely experienced anything but kindness, generosity, and warmth. On one occasion, a friend even left her very expensive camera behind and a local man ran after her departing bus to restore it to its rightful owner!

So be savvy, but not paranoid. Relax a little and trust your judgment. Accept kindness and invitations with good grace, and you'll quickly reap the rewards.

Keep on smiling

If you smile and are polite, you're far more likely to get a good reaction from people—as you do at home. Even if people are not being polite in return, you can often win them over with charm and good humor. This is a much better tactic than attempting to equal them in antagonism or aggressiveness. The service culture is very different to that at home—slow or even rude—but rather than bust a blood vessel about it, point it out calmly, and with the traveler's best companion—a smile.

6 Fearless Communications & happy homecoming

"No one realizes how beautiful it is to travel until he comes home and rests his head on his old, familiar pillow."

LIN YUTANG

Traveling gives you the thrill of experiencing countries and cultures totally removed from your own. But even when leaving civilization behind to trek into Outer Mongolia or plunge into the Amazonian rainforest, you'll still have one foot in your home country. So, unless you become the kind of veteran hobo that uproots his or her whole life to stay on the road, you'll want to stay in touch with what's happening at home.

I spend a great deal of time on the road, and I work hard to stay in touch with my loved ones and business associates back home. You, too, will probably want to think about the best ways to communicate with family and work while you're away.

For better or worse, most of us will be going back home eventually. So the fearless tips in this chapter will help you stay in touch when you're away, as well as enabling you to hang on to your precious memories and enjoy them for as long as possible once you're back in the comfort of your own living room.

THE WIRED TRAVELER

Options for staying in touch with home are more plentiful than ever before, but for the uninitiated, they become more confusing by the day. Whether you're a techno-whiz or totally baffled by megabytes, the potential value of technology to travelers is enormous.

Cellular phones

Staying in touch while on the road took an enormous leap forward with the cellular phone. If you're carrying a cell, your friends and family will always be able to call and check that you're OK and vice versa. You won't have to carry a pocketful of loose change to use expensive payphones or pay sky-high fees to use hotel phone lines. And aside from being able to communicate with telephones across the globe, the latest cellular phones are also personal organizers, radios, music players, voice recorders, cameras, and can even work as a video recorder—you can send an instant postcard or home video to everyone back home.

Energy efficiency

Finding the nearest electric outlet to charge your phone can be a real hassle. Fortunately, there are some clever solutions these days. There are solar-powered batteries and windup chargers—just two and a half spins per second for three minutes gives around eight hours of battery life. This is handy when you're miles from the nearest electric connection.

You can find and store local information on your cell if it has an Internet connection. You might want to keep a subway map handy, send e-mails, download maps to local campsites, receive news and traffic updates, and so on. The latest generation of GPS networks will soon be able to track your position and guide you to the nearest restaurant or ATM, simply through your phone.

On a different frequency

Did you know that your cell phone might not work abroad? The mishmash of different cell phone providers and technology around the world means that American phones often refuse to work in Europe and vice versa. So check out the capabilities of your cell phone before bringing it along. If it has CDMA or TDMA technology, chances are it won't function in Europe. Most European phones use GSM technology, which is also available in the US, but there's a big catch. The systems operate on a different bandwidth. So what's the solution? Well you could try to find a "tri-band" cell phone, which operates on all three GSM bandwidths, meaning that they work in just about every country. At present, they aren't common in the US but they are becoming increasingly available.

Alternatively, you can always buy a phone in the country you're visiting. That way, you won't pay for incoming calls—with a US-based number you'll have to pay sky-high fees when folks call you—and you'll pay much less for any local calls you make. But there's another clever solution for short trips. You can rent a new phone, either in your home country or when you reach your destination. Two US-based companies, www.cellularabroad.com and www.rent-a-cellphone.com, organize and supply cell-phone rentals or purchases abroad. Alternatively, you can organize your new phone when you reach your destination—you'll find booths offering rental phones at many major international airports.

Calling charges

Cell phones are fantastically versatile tools, but they can be expensive. For starters, making calls from abroad on a cell can quickly suck your wallet dry. Before setting off, call your service supplier to find out how much their international roaming charges are. Be warned—they are usually sky high.

It's a good idea to save your cell phone for emergencies and incoming calls—remember to keep these short because it's common for you to be charged for them too. Instead of routinely using your cell as you might at home, buy and use international phone cards to use on public phones and land lines anywhere. You'll be able to make international calls at the calling card's cheaper rates and simply pay for local calls. Some travelers also recommend using pre-paid cards on cell phones for similar reasons. Or find a cheap call shop. These are common in many parts of the world.

Satellite phones

Unlike cell phones, satellite phones should work from every square inch of the earth's surface without your having to wonder if your cell network covers an area. But they have not caught on very quickly. Their initial appeal quickly waned thanks to price tags of around $2000, high calling charges, and their sheer size—early models were sometimes as big as a briefcase. However, the industry is dropping its prices, size, and calling rates. If this trend continues, they may become a practical choice for fearless travelers with moderate means.

Laptops

The average fearless traveler has no real need to haul a laptop overseas, but business travelers who take them discover that they offer a bottomless well of resources. They can store data, pictures, videos, and games, as well as giving you instant access to the World Wide Web and e-mail accounts.

Portability is the laptop's great advantage. The internal battery lets you work unplugged for two hours or more, and you can extend this time by using another battery. So you can make every journey productive—no excuses.

The latest wireless technologies, combined with cell phone connectivity, allow you to exchange information between devices and connect to the Internet without cables or plugging into a phone line. Imagine yourself surfing the Web for a roadmap online as you're being driven down the highway, or checking the latest weather reports from your mountain chalet.

Plugging in

If you don't have the latest wireless technology on your laptop, you'll need to carry an Ethernet connector with you to access the Internet. Many high quality hotels now offer high-speed Internet connections, so you can simply plug into the line and you're off. Ask if you'll need a telephone adapter—plug styles differ around the world and the one you got with your laptop might not be appropriate for connections abroad. It's also a good idea to bring a long telephone cord so you can stretch it to wherever you feel most comfortable working.

E-mailing from laptops

Connecting to your home or work e-mail from a laptop can be a tricky process. Ask if your ISP has an access number that can be reached from where you're going, either through a toll-free number or a local number so you don't have to pay international rates. But be warned—your service provider will still charge extra when you access your account from overseas.

Given that what seemed impossible a decade ago is now an everyday reality in the computing world, you'll want to keep up to speed. The world of laptop travel changes quickly, so make a regular visit to such useful Websites as www.roadnews.com and www.kropla.com for the latest tips and recommendations.

A fragile pet

A laptop is a sensitive piece of engineering that has a lot of natural enemies, including heat, magnetism, water, sand, and humidity. It requires some tender loving care to protect it on the road. For example, humidity can create condensation and even mold in the electronic circuits or on the surface of the hard disk. Your laptop avoids overheating with a small internal fan. However, in hot countries this small fan may not be able to cool it sufficiently. If not, it will suffer from infuriating power cuts while you're working. Try to avoid this by working for only short periods of time and also by propping it up to allow hot air to escape more easily from below. It's worth taking these preventative measures, because heat can damage both your processor and your hard disc.

Lighter travel gizmos

If you don't want to carry a hefty laptop halfway across the globe, you can always settle for a smaller PDA or Pocket PC. This is generally how I work when I'm traveling. A pocket PC fulfils most of my needs when I'm on the road. PDAs and Pocket PCs are essentially computerized organizers, but also have the capability to store information and music, run familiar software programs, and connect to the Internet through compatible cell phones. They use a stylus pen as opposed to a keyboard—although compact, foldable keyboards are available—and some even have voice recognition capability and respond to verbal commands.

Create a travel blog

If you don't already have your own website, you can set up what is called a "travel blog" or "web log." This is basically geek-speak for a pre-programmed personal travel website. It may sound scary but it's actually beautifully simple to use. Just by following the instructions on the site, you can add diary entries and pictures to the site and show your route on a map, for all to see. And you can do this any time you like, from any Internet cafe, anywhere in the world.

Once you've written your update, an e-mail is automatically sent to everyone on your friends list. They can then click a link in the e-mail, visit the website, read the new text, view the photos, and follow your progress on a map. Simple!

A travel blog also creates an automatic back-up of your digital photos and travel journal. I've known people who lost their cameras, photos and journals while moving around—and it's a heartbreaking loss. But with a travel blog, the information can't be lost or stolen. Simply download the website when you get home and you have your complete illustrated travel journal.

To sample or set up a travel blog, visit one of these websites: *www.whereareyounow.com, www.deartraveldiary.com, www.mytripjournal.com,* or *www.yourtraveljournal.com.*

Over and out

Some instant-messaging applications, such as MSN
Messenger (www.msn.com), have a voice communication
option through which you can talk live with friends and family
back home. This is no more expensive than checking your
e-mails, so it's a very cheap way to reassure your family you're
safe when you're thousands of miles away.

This is how it works. Both you and the person you want to
talk to have to be connected to the Internet and logged into the
same messenger program. You'll both need a microphone and
headphones, but most Internet cafes have these accessories
today. Some programs, such as iChat (www.ichat.com), have
a video function as well, so if both parties have a web-cam,
you can actually see each other.

I just called to say...

So-called "net-to-phone" services are provided by several
websites. These allow you to call any telephone in the world
from a computer. It gives you far more freedom because you
don't have to agree on a time to call or to arrange a time when
both parties are logged onto the Internet. The other person
doesn't even need a computer. With an Internet connection, a
headset or microphone, and speakers, you're set to call the
other side of the world. The web provides a huge choice of
net-to-phone providers, but start with the following websites:
http://web.net2phone.com, http://www.mygo2call.com/
and http://www.iconnecthere.com/.

INTERNET CAFES

Dropping into the local Internet cafe to check e-mails is now the simplest thing in the world. Internet access has exploded worldwide, and even tiny towns far away from civilization are fast connecting to the Web. These days, it's a fair bet that there will be an Internet connection wherever there's a telephone line. E-mail is a cheap and quick way to send messages home, but it can also be a sophisticated tool for the traveler. So it's no surprise that Internet cafés are Meccas for travelers who like to stay in touch, record a diary of their trips, send home information, or chat online with travel buddies.

All your accounts in one

It's common for e-mail users to have a home/work e-mail account and a free web-based e-mail service such as Yahoo or Hotmail for traveling. However, you can also use these free services to check your other e-mail accounts. All you need to set this up is your account information; just follow the instructions on the free e-mail website. Even without an intermediary web-based e-mail, you can often check your home mail POP3 programs—Outlook Express, for example—abroad through an ISP website. Check with your service provider for information specific to your account before heading off. Normally, you just need a web address and your account information, and bingo, you're set. The only problem is that you no longer have an excuse not to read your office e-mail!

A locker in cyber space

One of the best things about e-mail is that you can safeguard important information in a place where it can't be lost, stolen, or forgotten. Take full advantage of this and use your traveling e-mail to hold vital travel information. Note important dates, numbers, and other details; think about scanning a few travel documents too, then simply e-mail everything to yourself to file away so you can retrieve it in case of an emergency.

Your e-mail account is also ideal for storing contacts— names, e-mail and home addresses, and telephone numbers. Some web-based e-mails also provide a Virtual Briefcase where you can store any kind of files—copies of documents, travel stories, local music recordings, or anything else. And if that isn't generous enough, you can also have a Virtual Photo Album for storing your digital vacation photos. You can order prints online, so it's possible to have them waiting in your mailbox even before you're back from your trip.

Happy birthday from afar

Going to miss someone's birthday while traveling and want to send a card? Postal systems around the world can be a tad unpredictable, to say the least. It's common for your postcards to arrive well after you're home. I once sent my grandmother a postcard at my first port of call on a five-month trip and it arrived a month after I had returned! So, it's a good idea to drop into your nearest internet cafe and send a back-up E-card to make sure at least one arrives on the day.

NETWORKING WITH TRAVELERS

Every destination has its upsides, downsides, challenges, and hidden secrets. And all destinations are constantly changing, so it's vital to keep up and know what to expect. The best way to prepare and keep track of what's going on is to stay in touch with fellow travelers—people who've been there, done that, scaled the mountain, and cruised the cruise. They'll have a good idea of the challenges and adventures open to you and will have all kinds of insider information about ways to approach them.

Online travel forums

There are plenty of online travel discussion groups called forums, newsgroups, or conferences, as well as mailing lists for all the latest travel gossip and updates. Newsgroups and forums work like a cork bulletin board where people leave notes, newspaper clippings, photos, and other items. Each time you walk by the board, you can check what's new and who has replied to the last note you left. Just go to the web address to post messages and check for replies. Some e-mail programs can also deliver new postings straight to your inbox. Lonely Planet's ThornTree (http://thorntree.lonelyplanet.com/) is one of the biggest and most popular worldwide travel forums. Also try Travel Talk on http://travel.roughguides.com or http://frommers.com which also has a wide range of message boards in their community.

Staying in touch with fearless friends

Like-minded folk quickly hook up on the road and end up sharing memories. So why not set up an e-mail group to make sure you keep in touch? Yahoo Groups is a popular free service available at http://groups.yahoo.com. Every message each member posts here goes to everybody in the gang.

Imagine that you plan to hike a centuries-old Inca trail to a newly discovered lost city in the Andes but don't know how to go about it. Simply post a message in the forum and wait for savvy traveler tips and comments to come rolling your way. It's just as if you had a panel of travel experts ready to solve every travel dilemma or worry.

PRESERVING YOUR MEMORIES

Travel should be an adventure you'll never forget, and vivid moments will undoubtedly stick with you for ever. Here are some tips to make sure you can relive memories of your trip time and again once you're home.

Daily journal

The most treasured possessions that I own are my diaries from various marathon trips around Asia and Latin America. I have an image of myself when I'm old, wrapped in a blanket in a comfy armchair, chuckling over my old travel journals.

Writing a journal is the ideal way to document all those quirky, teling little details that you can't remember from photos, guidebooks, and memory alone.

Here you can put your stream of thought in writing and actually express what it felt like to swim in that waterfall, sleep in a hammock, stroke a wild tarantula, or just how you befriended the local cab driver and met his grandmother for tea. It's also the ideal way to absorb and internalize your day's excitement—just take 10 minutes each night to scribble down your stories, adventures, insights, and impressions of everything around you. Years from now, you'll be so glad you did!

Don't write exclusively about the big stuff. Include everyday things, too—the quirky differences in culture and food, funny things that happen, colorful characters, and unusual sights. If the high-speed bus rattling dangerously along a mountainside has a religious "Christ will save us" sticker on the windshield, say so. Note down odd place names—for example Bally Seedy Garden Center in Ireland—and unusual sights such as brightly packaged love potions in the market. Anything that makes you stop and chuckle is worth remembering.

Musical memories

Music has a singular knack of transporting you back to a particular time and place. I, for one, can't hear salsa or cumbia music without visualizing myself bouncing along a dirt track in a Latin American bus or being whirled around the dance floor.

So treat yourself to buying or recording some favorite music tracks that you'll always associate with your trip. Listen to them when you get home and you'll feel the memories come flooding back.

An image is worth...

Taking photos or videos as a record of your various escapades is a great way to immortalize your experiences. They inspire travel memories more surely than any other medium. You have a huge choice of cameras to take on your travels, including everything from credit-card-sized digital cameras to video camcorders and disposable plastic cameras to more serious professional-quality single lens reflex cameras (SLRs) complete with lenses, filters, and accessories. Digital cameras are now the best way to send photos back home and also let you back up your precious vacation snaps on the Internet.

Be aware that you might run into trouble if you try to take pictures of religious sites, military installations, or secure places such as airports. Police and military personnel can be quite touchy about this. I once got hauled in front of the police superintendent in India simply for making notes on a clipboard outside his police station.

Sharing the shutter

If you're traveling with a good friend, consider sharing camera duties. You could take one camera or take turns carrying it for the day. This way you can avoid taking the same shots and printing redundant copies of each other's film when you return home.

But even better, splitting the responsibility will often free you from looking at the world "through the lens of a camera," or to put it another way, you won't have to be constantly watching for a good photo. But no matter what, remember to step back, relax, and absorb everything through your own eyes every once in a while.

Going home

Coming home can be a wonderful feeling if you've been missing loved ones and creature comforts. Once you're home and have relaxed into familiar surroundings, you can also appreciate a full sense of achievement from your trip.

But along with bringing a sense of completion and achievement, coming home can inspire all kinds of other emotions in the fearless traveler—reluctance or sadness at leaving, a craving to discover more, and perhaps a certain culture shock or detachment when returning to your everyday life. Perhaps you've caught the travel bug and you simply don't want to stop.

The being-back-home blues can kick in when you least expect it, but fortunately, there are ways to minimize them.

Relive your travels as much as possible. Jot down stories about the people you met and things you saw and did while they're fresh in your mind. Write or phone friends you made along the way and arrange photos in an album with notes on the back. If you feel really inspired, you could even compose some stories about your adventures to post on travel websites or to sell to magazines. Whatever methods you choose, you'll be keeping the memory of your experience alive.

Keep on walking...

However, at the end of the day, the surest way to beat the back-home blues is simple. You have to go on feeding your addiction—if only in the imagination. The travel bug is, I'm happy to say, an incurable disease. If you're anything like me, you'll start planning and saving for your next adventure immediately on touchdown. The more you discover, the more you'll want to discover. So give in to the urges of your itchy feet: inspire yourself with new dreams, experiences, and knowledge. Keep on broadening your mind with the travel drug. The world out there is just waiting for you to explore its endless complexity and possibilities, so why keep it waiting?

Good luck and happy fearless travels!

Index

Core Packing List

This list contains many of the most basic travel items for your kit. However, everybody's needs are different, so add and subtract your own packing ideas and customize the list to suit each destination.

- [ ] Backpack/Suitcase
- [ ] Daypack
- [ ] Money belt
- [ ] Plastic bags
- [ ] Water bottle
- [ ] Universal drain plug
- [ ] Padlocks
- [ ] Pocketknife
- [ ] Flashlight
- [ ] Clothesline or string
- [ ] Sewing kit
- [ ] Cup and spoon
- [ ] Compass
- [ ] Camera and film
- [ ] Novel
- [ ] Guidebook
- [ ] Journal/notebook
- [ ] Address list
- [ ] Shoes: one pair light, one tougher
- [ ] Socks
- [ ] Trousers, one pair zip-off
- [ ] Optional skirt
- [ ] Shirts, blouses, T-shirts
- [ ] Underwear
- [ ] Hat
- [ ] Sweater

- [ ] Rain jacket, umbrella
- [ ] Swimwear
- [ ] Sarong
- [ ] Bandanna
- [ ] Sunglasses
- [ ] Thermals
- [ ] Toothbrush and paste
- [ ] Travel towel
- [ ] Soap and dish
- [ ] Shampoo
- [ ] Toilet paper
- [ ] Comb or brush
- [ ] Small plastic mirror
- [ ] Earplugs
- [ ] Safety pins
- [ ] Razor and blades
- [ ] Sunscreen
- [ ] Insect repellent
- [ ] Band Aids
- [ ] First-aid kit
- [ ] Folding scissors
- [ ] Water purification chemicals or pump
- [ ] Painkillers
- [ ] Lip balm
- [ ] Diarrhea tablets
- [ ] Motion sickness tablets